# Quick Work

*Workbook*

David Grant

Great Clarendon Street, Oxford OX2 6DP

Oxford University Press is a department of the University of Oxford. It furthers the University's objective of excellence in research, scholarship, and education by publishing worldwide in

Oxford New York

Auckland Bangkok Buenos Aires Cape Town Chennai
Dar es Salaam Delhi Hong Kong Istanbul Karachi Kolkata
Kuala Lumpur Madrid Melbourne Mexico City Mumbai Nairobi
São Paulo Shanghai Taipei Tokyo Toronto

Oxford and Oxford English are registered trade marks of Oxford University Press in the UK and in certain other countries

© Oxford University Press 2002

The moral rights of the author have been asserted

Database right Oxford University Press (maker)

First published 2002
Second impression 2003

**No unauthorized photocopying**

All rights reserved. No part of this publication may be reproduced, stored in a retrieval system, or transmitted, in any form or by any means, without the prior permission in writing of Oxford University Press, or as expressly permitted by law, or under terms agreed with the appropriate reprographics rights organization. Enquiries concerning reproduction outside the scope of the above should be sent to the ELT Rights Department, Oxford University Press, at the address above

You must not circulate this book in any other binding or cover and you must impose this same condition on any acquirer

Any websites referred to in this publication are in the public domain and their addresses are provided by Oxford University Press for information only. Oxford University Press disclaims any responsibilty for the content.

ISBN 0 19 457290 0

Printed in Hong Kong

**Acknowledgements**

The authors and publisher are grateful to those who have given permission to reproduce the following extracts and adaptations of copyright material:

p18 'Forecourt ad firm plans float' by Dominic Rush © Times Newspapers Ltd 10 September 2000. Reproduced by permission of Times Newspapers Ltd.

p37 Extracts from 'How to complain about Muzak in the UK' by Terry Birchmore. Reproduced by permission of Terry Birchmore.

**Sources:**

p12 Information taken from the Swedish Tourist Board website: www.sverigeturism.se
pp14, 15 Information taken from www.vivendi.com
p28 Information taken from www.mikkis.co.uk
p32 Information taken from The Economist Pocket World in Figures 2000

Illustrations supplied by:
Mark Duffin pp25, 46
Tim Kahane pp7, 28
Nigel Paige pp10, 26, 37
Viv Quillin pp17, 27, 47

The publishers would like to thank the following for their kind permission to reproduce photographs and copyright material:

Michelin p5
Nestlé p5
Financial Times Picture Library p32 (truck)
Forecourt TV p18 (man filling car with petrol)
Image Bank p11 (business people meeting), 12 (businessmen wearing football helmets)
Photographers Library p4 (woman meeting businessmen), p35 (business woman)
Popperfoto p21 (J M Keynes)
Psion p42 (Revo Plus)
Robert Harding p6 (airport scene)
Still Pictures p32 (Mark Dickinson/traffic jam, Adrian Arbib 2H/overcrowded truck, NRSC/freeway multiple junction, Peter Frischmuth/autobahn and railway)
Jeffrey Tabberner p32 (Indian street scene)
zoom.co.uk p19 (web page)
Cover: Railman Photo Office (train) and Photodisc

Although every effort has been made to trace and contact copyright holders before publication, this has not always been possible. We apologize for any apparent infringement of copyright and if notified the publisher will be pleased to rectify any errors or omissions at the earliest opportunity.

Designed by Jeffrey Tabberner

## CONTENTS

**1** Out and about 4

**2** Presenting your company 14

**3** Exchanging information 24

**4** Getting things done 34

**5** Planning ahead 44

    Language reference 52

    Answer key 58

## Out and about

### 1 GETTING TO KNOW YOU

**Language reference 1 and 7, pp52 and 54**

Complete the questions **1–7**, then match them to the answers **a–g**. See the example.

1 Who __do__ you work __for__ ?
2 What _____ you do?
3 Where _____ your company based?
4 What _____ your company _____ ?
5 What nationality _____ you?
6 Where _____ you work?
7 What languages _____ you speak?

a In Kyoto.
b I'm Japanese.
c English and a little Spanish.
d Mashui Electronics.
e I'm a Project Manager.
f In the Kyoto office.
g We produce electronic components.

### 2 ANSWERING QUESTIONS

Now answer the questions in 1–7 above for yourself.

1 _I work for ..._
2 _____
3 _____
4 _____
5 _____
6 _____
7 _____

## 3 COUNTRIES AND NATIONALITIES

Where are these companies based? What nationality are the people from that country? Complete the table with words from this list. See the example.

*France*  *Korea*  *Spanish*  *Switzerland*  *USA*  *Germany*
*Japanese*  *Dutch*  *French*  *German*  *Korean*  *Japan*
*Spain*  *Holland*  *Swiss*  *American*

  TOSHIBA

| COMPANY | COUNTRY | NATIONALITY |
|---|---|---|
| 1 Michelin | France | French |
| 2 Nestlé | | |
| 3 BMW | | |
| 4 Philips | | |
| 5 Repsol | | |
| 6 Toshiba | | |
| 7 Hyundai | | |
| 8 Intel | | |

## 4 QUESTIONS OF NATIONALITY

**Language reference 1 and 7, pp52 and 54**

Complete these questions and answers. See the example.

1. A Where ___do___ you work?
   B In Rome. I work for an ___Italian___ company.

2. A Where _____ they come from?
   B They come from Lisbon. They're P_____.

3. A Who _____ he work for?
   B For Ericsson, in Sweden. It's a S_____ company.

4. A Where _____ your new boss from?
   B She's from Toronto. She's C_____.

5. A Where _____ he work?
   B He works in Poland, but he doesn't speak P_____.

6. A What languages _____ you speak in your company?
   B We speak English and we also speak S_____ because our company's based in Argentina.

Out and about

## 5 AIRPORT SERVICES

a   Match the words in **1–8** with those in **a–h** to give the names of eight airport services and facilities. See the example.

1 check-in — a toilets
2 car          b aid
3 information  c luggage
4 gift         d lounge
5 men's        e shop
6 first        f desk
7 left         g hire
8 departure    h area

b   Now choose one of the services/facilities in **a** to complete each sentence.

1  I want to buy a present for my husband in the _____ _____.
2  If you fall and cut yourself you can go to the _____ _____ room.
3  If you arrive early at the airport, you can leave your suitcase at _____ _____ and go shopping.
4  I'm going to the _____ _____ to wash my hands.
5  You can ask about hotels at the _____ _____.
6  A  Excuse me, where do I register for a Johannesburg flight?
   B  The _____ _____ for all international departures is on the first floor.
7  The _____ _____ desk is closed for the evening – I think I'll take a taxi to the hotel and rent a car tomorrow.
8  Shall we go through to the _____ _____ to wait for our flight?

Out and about

## 6 DESCRIBING A FACTORY

The Production Manager of a company is showing a visitor the main factory. They are standing at point **X** on the plan below.

a Read what the Production Manager says and write the names of the different parts of the factory 1–6.

*OK, so this is the factory. Directly on the left here there's a store for equipment. Just opposite the store, on your right, there's the packing room, where we put all the finished products in boxes. Just next to the packing room there's the testing area where we check the finished product. The cutting machines are over there behind the testing area. On the left, next to the equipment room, is the preparation area – this is where we prepare all the different parts. And between the preparation area and the cutting machines there's the main production area …*

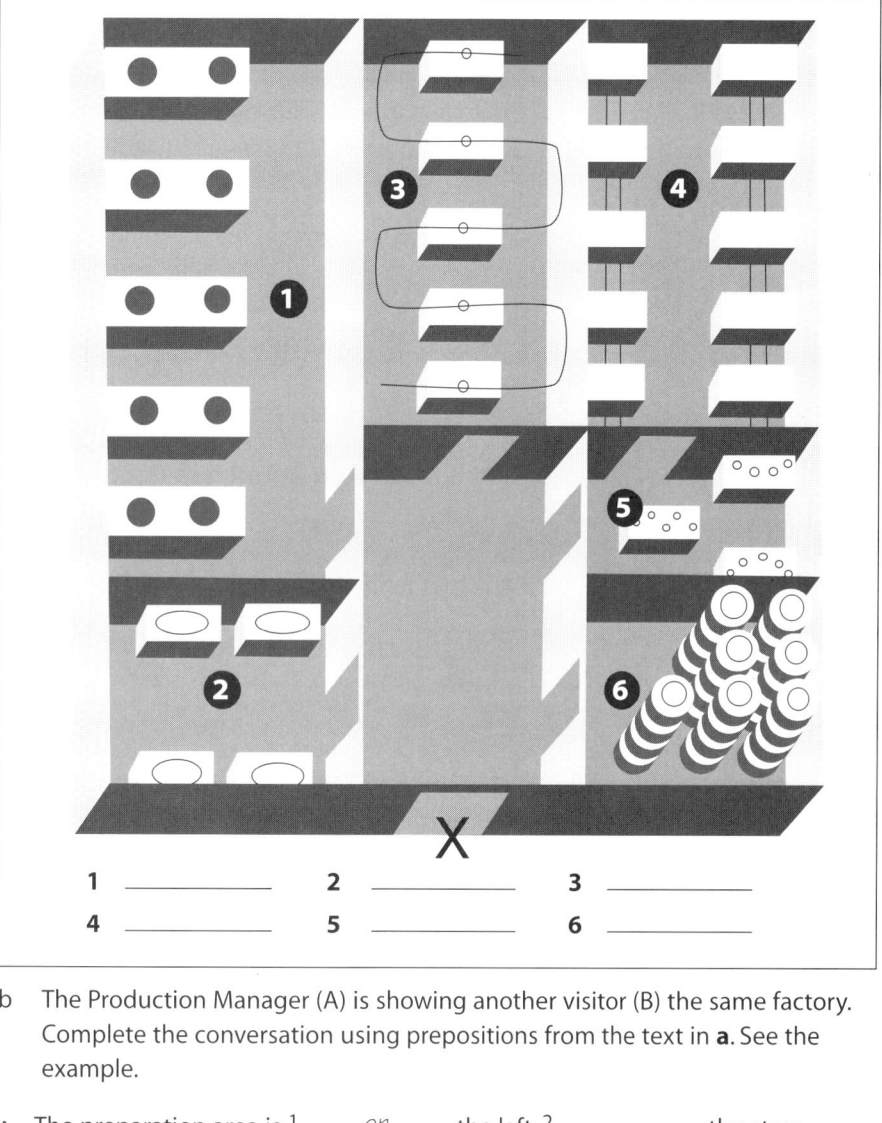

1 _____  2 _____  3 _____
4 _____  5 _____  6 _____

b The Production Manager (A) is showing another visitor (B) the same factory. Complete the conversation using prepositions from the text in **a**. See the example.

A The preparation area is [1] __on__ the left, [2] _____ the store. The production area is [3] _____ _____ the preparation area, and the cutting machines are on the [4] _____.

B Where's the testing area?

A It's there, [5] _____ the cutting machines and the packing room.

B And what about your office?

A It's not in this building. It's just [6] _____ the factory, [7] _____ there on the other side of the road.

Out and about

7

## 7 CONFERENCE DETAILS

**Language reference 1 and 7, pp52 and 54**

Use this conference programme to complete each question **1–8** then answer the questions. Write complete sentences for the answers. See the example.

### Conference programme

**Friday April 12 – Final morning**

9.30 a.m.   Talk by Robert L. Payton

10.15 a.m.  Coffee

10.30 a.m.  Bus tour of Washington
**or** Visit to Air and Space Museum
Buses for both tours leave from front of hotel

1.00 p.m.   Buffet lunch in Cactus Cantina restaurant (next to hotel). Closes at 2.30 p.m.

Minibus from hotel to Dulles Airport every half hour from 2.10 p.m. to 5.40 p.m. Journey time approximately 45 minutes.

1   What time does the talk start?
    *It starts at half past nine/nine-thirty.*

2   _____ there a coffee break in the morning?

3   _____ there any talks or presentations after the coffee break?

4   What time _____ the buses leave for the morning tours?

5   Where _____ the buses leave from?

6   What time _____ the Cactus Cantina close?

7   Where _____ the Cactus Cantina?

8   What time _____ the first minibus arrive at Dulles airport?

**Out and about**

## 8 ALPHABET SOUP

Choose letters which have the same sound as these words. See the example.

| pl**ay** | b**e** | b**e**d | fl**y** | n**o** | y**ou** | st**ar** |
|---|---|---|---|---|---|---|
| _ _ _ | E _ _ | M _ | _ _ | _ | _ _ | _ |

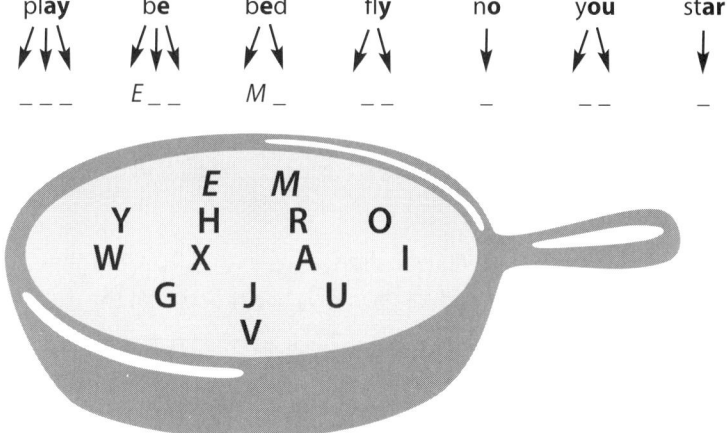

## 9 TELEPHONE REQUESTS

*Language reference 14, p56*

Complete the questions in the conversation below by using an expression from **A** and a word or phrase from **B**. See the example.

| A | B |
|---|---|
| Could you | take |
| Can I | spell that |
|  | repeat |
|  | have the name of |
|  | speak to |
|  | give me |
|  | **help you** |

A  FTS. Good morning. ¹ _Can I help you?_

B  Hello. ² _____ your Purchasing Manager, please?

A  Yes, of course. His name's Monsieur Arrouet.

B  Sorry. ³ _____, please?

A  Yes. It's A-double R-O-U-E-T.

B  Thank you. ⁴ _____ Monsieur Arrouet, please?

A  I'm sorry, but he's in a meeting. ⁵ _____ a message?

B  No, that's OK, thank you. ⁶ _____ his direct phone number?

A  I'm afraid that's not possible. But I have his secretary's number. It's 01 32 58 97 44.

B  Sorry, ⁷ _____ the last four numbers?

A  Yes, that's 97 44.

B  OK, thanks very much. Goodbye.

Out and about

## 10 INVITATIONS

Language reference 13, pp55–6

Complete these invitations. See the examples. Sometimes you need a verb (as in **1**), sometimes a noun (as in **2**).

1  Would you like ___to use___ the microphone for your talk?
2  A  Would you like ___a cigarette___?
   B  No thanks, I don't smoke.
3  Would you like _____ my newspaper? I've finished with it.
4  A  I need to send an e-mail.
   B  Would you like _____ my computer?
5  I'm afraid Mr Carrera is in a meeting at the moment. Would you like _____ back later?
6  A  Would you like _____?
   B  Yes, please. Black with no sugar.
7  Would you like _____ for dinner this evening?
8  A  Would you like _____ of this report?
   B  Thanks, but I already have a copy in my office.

## 11 SOCIAL RESPONSES

Language reference 13, p55–6

Match sentences **1–8** with responses **a–h**.

1  Nice to see you again.              a  You're welcome.
2  I'm sorry I'm late.                 b  I'm sorry to hear that.
3  Please have a seat.                 c  You too.
4  Could I make a phone call?          d  Thanks.
5  Thanks very much.                   e  It's no problem.
6  I'm afraid I can't come.            f  Thanks. Here?
7  Would you like something to drink?  g  Of course. Go ahead.
8  Here you are.                       h  Yes, please.

Out and about

## 12 JOB RESPONSIBILITIES

The CEO of a company is introducing two of his managers to a visitor. Complete the descriptions. The first letter of each word is given.

*This is our Quality Manager, Julie Brost. She ¹r_____ t_____ me. She's ²r_____ f_____ improving the quality of our production and administrative systems. She ³m_____ a team of five people.*

*And can I introduce you to our other Chief Engineer, Mario Koplowitz. He's ⁴i_____ c_____ o_____ new product development. He also ⁵m_____ our new electronics division. He ⁶r_____ t_____ the Production Manager.*

## 13 YOU AND YOUR JOB

Now write sentences about yourself.

1  I'm a/the _____.

2  I'm in charge of _____.

3  I'm also responsible for _____.

4  I report to _____.

Out and about

11

## 14 MANAGEMENT CULTURE

Read the text and say if the statements below are true (T) or false (F). Write your answers in column **A**. Then complete column **B** for your country or company.

|  | A<br>Sweden | B<br>My country/<br>company |
|---|---|---|
| 1 There aren't many levels of management. | ____ | ____ |
| 2 It is easy to make decisions. | ____ | ____ |
| 3 Managers like to make all the decisions. | ____ | ____ |
| 4 Employees know what's happening in the company. | ____ | ____ |
| 5 Managers don't get angry or excited in meetings. | ____ | ____ |
| 6 Managers like to show that they are the boss. | ____ | ____ |
| 7 Managers are often younger than non-managers. | ____ | ____ |

# Management in Sweden

Swedish companies usually have a simple management structure. The result is a simple and direct decision-making process.

Swedish employees on all levels are free to solve problems without talking to their superiors. The Swedish style of management is based on the idea that the individual wants to and can do a good job. A Swedish manager thinks of himself as a sports coach more than a military commander, and he often delegates work to his staff.

The Swedes consider that a good manager is a person who uses the natural creativity and motivation of his staff. The Swedish manager always informs his team of what is happening in the company. In meetings, it is important to be a good listener, and not to get emotional when discussing a problem.

Managers and their employees normally call each other by their first names. Managers treat their employees as equals. Managers also accept it if members of their team make decisions without them. In Swedish companies, decisions are made to achieve a result and not to show your position in the company.

In many countries, management positions are given to the older staff. In Sweden, work performance is usually more important. As a result, young men and women are often seen in top positions.

| | |
|---|---|
| **creativity** | the ability to make new things or have new ideas |
| to **delegate** | to ask members of your team to do parts of your job for you |
| **emotional** | showing your feelings too much |
| as **equals** | having the same level/position (in the company) |
| **motivation** | a desire to do something |

Out and about

## 15 CROSSWORD

Complete the crossword. All the words appear in Unit 1.

**Across**

1 Please come in and have a _____.
2 She works _____ Mitsubishi.
5 He's an _____ in the Technical Department.
7 The company is _____ in Chicago, Illinois.
11 Could I _____ your passport, please?
13 Excuse me. What time does the plane from Oslo _____?
14 I work in Research _____ Development.

**Down**

1 The _____ Manager is responsible for selling the company's products.
3 This shop _____ at 8.30 in the morning.
4 General Motors _____ cars.
6 Would you like to _____ on a tour of the company?
8 He's _____ architect.
9 Can you help me? _____ there a telephone near here?
10 Where's your company's _____ office?
12 Five forty-five is the same as quarter to _____.

Out and about

13

# 2 Presenting your company

## 1 TRADING AREAS

Match two countries from this list with each trading area in **1–6**. See the example.

| **Great Britain** | Thailand | Argentina | Hungary |
|---|---|---|---|
| Canada | Poland | Saudi Arabia | Brazil |
| Portugal | USA | Egypt | Vietnam |

1 Western Europe      *Great Britain*      _____
2 Eastern Europe      _____          _____
3 The Middle East     _____          _____
4 South-East Asia     _____          _____
5 North America       _____          _____
6 South America       _____          _____

## 2 COMPANY ACTIVITIES

a Find the words and expressions in **1–8** in the text below and the table opposite, then match them with definitions **a–h**.

1 employees          a to own more than 50% of the capital
2 general public     b numbers
3 plants             c names of products or groups of products
4 majority share     d volume of sales (in £, $, €, etc.)
5 waste treatment    e people who work for a company
6 figures            f ordinary people, not companies
7 brands             g processing/recycling of things we don't need
8 turnover           h factories

### Vivendi Universal

**Vivendi Universal** *is a global media and communications company. It also has a majority share in* **Vivendi Environnement**, *the world leader in environmental services. Here are some key facts and figures, as well as the names of some of the companies or brands in each operating division.*

Presenting your company

14

| | Division/sector | Turnover in € (2,000) | Employees | Companies/brands | Activities |
|---|---|---|---|---|---|
| **Vivendi Universal** | TV and film | 8.79 bn | 25,000 | Canal + Universal Studios | 1 *Operates* pay-TV channels 2 Pr_____ films for TV and cinema. |
| | Publishing | 3.6 bn | 22,000 | Flipside Larousse Nathan | 3 Pu_____ games, educational CD-roms, books and magazines. |
| | Music | 6.61 bn | 12,000 | Barclay Decca Deutsche Grammophon | 4 Ha_____ 22.5% of the world music market and a catalogue of 800,000 titles. |
| | Internet | *N/A | *N/A | Vizzavi.com Atmedica.com Education.com | 5 Pr_____ online information services; 6 De_____ websites for TV, publishing and music divisions. |
| | Telephone | 5.1 bn | 8,300 | SFR Cegetel | 7 Se_____ phone services to general public and business customers. |
| **Vivendi Environnement** | Environment | 26.51 bn | 220,000 | Vivendi Water Dalkia Onyx | 8 Co_____ and 9 op_____ water, energy and waste treatment plants. |

*N/A = information not available

b  Now complete the table by putting the correct verbs in the 'Activities' column. The first two letters are given. See the example.

Presenting your company

15

## 3 SAYING NUMBERS

*Language reference 16, pp56–7*

a  Write these numbers in figures. See the example.

1  twelve thousand — 12,000
2  twenty-two thousand — _____
3  eight hundred thousand — _____
4  six point six one billion — _____
5  twenty-two and a half — _____

b  These numbers are all from the table about the Vivendi companies on page 15 but they are not exact. Write the exact number in words. See the example.

1  about twenty per cent — twenty-two point five per cent (22.5%)
2  about two hundred thousand — _____
3  about nine billion — _____
4  about eight thousand — _____
5  about twenty-seven billion — _____

## 4 ASKING ABOUT QUANTITY

*Language reference 10, pp54–5*

a  Complete the questions **1–8** with *much* or *many*. Then match them with answers **a–h** below. See the example.

1  How __many__ hours a week do you work? ____
2  How _____ computers do you have at home and in your office? ____
3  How _____ wine or beer can you drink if you are driving? ____
4  How _____ mobile phones do you have in your family? ____
5  How _____ time do you spend watching TV every evening? ____
6  How _____ experience do you need to do your job? ____
7  How _____ meetings do you have every week? ____
8  How _____ money do you spend on petrol every month? ____

a  Only two small glasses in my country.
b  Five – one for me, one for my husband, and one for each of my children.
c  It depends on the week, but probably about three or four.
d  Between forty and fifty.
e  I've no idea. I have a company car and I pay with a company credit card.
f  About five or six years in sales or marketing.
g  I have one at work and a laptop, which I always carry with me.
h  No more than half an hour most evenings.

b  Now answer questions **1–8** for yourself.

Presenting your company

## 5 COMPANY DEPARTMENTS

Which departments in a company deal with products?

a   Complete the flowchart with the names of these departments.

*Packaging   Marketing   Customer Service   Advertising   Production*

Idea → Research And Development → 1_____ → Purchasing → 2_____ → Quality Control → 3_____ → Sales → 4_____ → Dispatch → Customer Accounts → 5_____

b   Which department in the flowchart:

1 buys the parts to make the product?   _____
2 sends the product to the customer?   _____
3 tests the idea with future customers?   _____
4 finds people to buy the product?   _____
5 informs the market about the product?   _____
6 asks customers to pay for the product?   _____

Presenting your company

17

## 6 PRESENT ACTIVITIES

**Language reference 1 and 2, p52**

a   Read the text and put the verbs in brackets into the Present simple or Present continuous. See the examples.

Tony Vickers, Chairman of FTV

What can you do while you're filling your car with petrol? Watch TV, of course! The advertising company FTV ¹ _is installing_ (install) television screens in 1,000 petrol stations in Great Britain. The screen ² _switches on_ (switch on) when someone ³_____ (start) using the petrol pump, and ⁴_____ (show) advertisements for products sold in that station. The company has signed contracts with Texaco and Total Fina Elf.

Tony Vickers, the Chairman of FTV, says that petrol stations always ⁵_____ (provide) a great audience for advertisers. About 1,200 people ⁶_____ (pass) through a busy petrol station every day. Most of these ⁷_____ (be) young and ⁸_____ (have) money to spend.

These days, petrol stations ⁹_____ (sell) more and more products like food, books and videos. At the same time, the big supermarket groups ¹⁰_____ (open) their own petrol stations. It's not difficult to see why petrol station advertising ¹¹_____ (become) more and more popular.

Alan Bryson, FTV Chief Executive, says the company ¹²_____ (talk) to other possible partners, including supermarket groups. The company also ¹³_____ (have) plans to move into Europe.

b   Write questions about the text. See the examples. Then answer them.

1   What/FTV/install?
    _What is FTV installing?_

2   When/screen/switch on?
    _When does the screen switch on?_

3   What/petrol stations/always/provide?
    _____

4   What/more and more petrol stations/sell?
    _____

5   What/big supermarket groups/do?
    _____

6   Who/FTV/talk/to?
    _____

7   What other plans/company/have?
    _____

Presenting your company

18

## 7 ACTIVE OR PASSIVE

*Language reference 8 and 17, pp54 and 57*

Choose the correct form of the verb in *italics*. See the example.

1 These parts *make*/**are made** in Portugal.
2 We *give/are given* all our customers a small gift every Christmas.
3 They *pack/are packed* their products in paper.
4 The order *confirms/is confirmed* by e-mail.
5 Where are these machines *sell/sold*?
6 The company *buys/is bought* all its parts from a Japanese supplier.
7 Every product *is/does* tested by an operator.
8 *Do/are* you deliver on a Saturday?
9 They *don't/aren't* send the goods if the invoice *isn't/doesn't* paid.

## 8 SHOPPING ONLINE

*Language reference 8 and 17, pp54 and 57*

Read the text about the Zoom online shopping service, then complete the notes. See the example.

## How do we process your order? → → → →

When you press the 'Buy' button, our computer automatically sends you an e-mail to confirm the order. Then it checks the stock position and your credit-card details. Next, it sends the order details to the warehouse. In the warehouse we have 'pickers' and 'packers'. The picker finds your products in the warehouse. Then, the packer packs them, puts the invoice in the box, and creates an address label. Finally, he sends you an e-mail confirming the delivery time and puts your package in the post. The whole process normally takes no more than 24 hours.

1 First, an e-mail *is sent to the customer to confirm the order*.
2 Then, the stock position and credit-card details _____.
3 Next, the order details _____.
4 In the warehouse, the products _____.
5 Then the products _____.
6 The invoice _____.
7 An address label _____.
8 Finally, _____.

Presenting your company

**Language reference 7, p54**

## 9 TO BE OR NOT TO BE

Morgana (M) phones her colleague Tom (T) on the way from Montreal to Toronto. Complete the gaps with the correct form of the verb be – is, were, wasn't, etc.

M  ¹_____ that Tom?

T  Yes, it ²_____. Hi, Morgana. Where ³_____ you?

M  I ⁴_____ on the motorway. I'm driving to Toronto.

T  Where ⁵_____ you this morning when I called? There ⁶_____ no answer.

M  I ⁷_____ at a product presentation in Montreal. It finished at twelve.

T  ⁸_____ there many people there?

M  No, there ⁹_____. And the CEO ¹⁰_____ there either!

T  That's a pity. He ¹¹_____ the most important person to see.

M  Yes, unfortunately. Tom, can you look on my desk?

T  Yes, OK.

M  ¹²_____ my glasses there?

T  No, they ¹³_____. There ¹⁴_____ anything on your desk.

M  OK, then I think they ¹⁵_____ probably still in my hotel room in Montreal.

T  Oh, dear. Is that a problem?

M  No, I can manage. Thanks for your help, Tom. Bye.

## 10 PERSONAL HISTORY

**Language reference 3 and 17, pp52–3 and 57**

a  How do you pronounce the *-ed* ending of the regular verbs in column **A**? Write /d/, /ɪd/ or /t/. See the example.

b  The verbs in column **B** are irregular. Write the past tense form. See the example.

| A | | B | |
|---|---|---|---|
| accepted | /ɪd/ | think | *thought* |
| worked | _____ | go | _____ |
| published | _____ | be | _____ |
| studied | _____ | write | _____ |
| started | _____ | teach | _____ |
| negotiated | _____ | have | _____ |
| returned | _____ | begin | _____ |
| joined | _____ | leave | _____ |

c  Complete the text opposite about John Maynard Keynes, the famous economist, using each verb in **A** and **B** once.

Presenting your company

20

# John Maynard Keynes
## *The man who changed economic theory*

Born in 1883, John Maynard Keynes ¹_____ Maths and Economics at Cambridge University. After his studies, he ²_____ for the Civil Service for a few years, then ³_____ to Cambridge, where he ⁴_____ students until 1915. When World War I ⁵_____ , he ⁶_____ the Civil Service again, where he ⁷_____ responsible for economic relations with the other countries at war.

After the war, he was very unhappy about the economic sanctions against Germany. In protest, he ⁸_____ his Civil Service job and then ⁹_____ his first famous essay 'The Economic Consequences of the Peace', published in 1919.

In the 1920s Keynes ¹⁰_____ that governments were wrong to do nothing about high unemployment. At that time he ¹¹_____ no economic theory to support his ideas, but in the mid-30s, he ¹²_____ 'The General Theory of Employment, Interest and Money'.
The world was now in economic crisis, and governments and politicians ¹³_____ to listen to Keynes' theories. During World War II and after, many Western democracies ¹⁴_____ his idea of maintaining high employment.

In 1945, at the end of his Civil Service career, Keynes ¹⁵_____ to the USA and ¹⁶_____ a multi-billion dollar loan for Great Britain. He died the following year.

| | |
|---|---|
| the **Civil Service** | general name for all government departments |
| **consequences** | things that are the result of something else |
| **crisis** | serious difficulty |
| **essay** | a (usually short) piece of writing on a subject |
| **high employment** | when a lot of people have a job |
| or **unemployment** | when a lot of people don't have a job |
| **loan** | money that you borrow and have to pay back later |
| **protest** | an action taken to show you don't agree with something |
| **sanctions** | actions taken to make a country follow international law |
| **theory** | a system of ideas to explain something |

Presenting your company

## 11 A JOB INTERVIEW

a  Write the questions for a job interview. See the example.

1  Who/you/work for? *Who do you work for?*
2  What sort of job/you/look for? _____
3  When/you/join/present company? _____
4  Where/your company/based? _____
5  What/your company/do? _____
6  Where/its products/sell? _____
7  Which department/you/work in? _____
8  What/you/work on at the moment? _____
9  Where/you/work before? _____
10 Why/you/leave/last job? _____

b  Now find answers to the questions in **1–10** above in the squares below. The answer to question 1 is in one of the squares touching the 'Start' square – **A**, **D**, or **E**.

If you think the answer to question 1 is **D**, then the answer to question 2 will be in square **A**, **E**, **H**, or **I**, and so on. If all your answers are correct, you will arrive at the 'Congratulations' square and get the job!

| **Start** interview here. | **A** My boss. | **B** In 1999. | **C** In 1903. |
|---|---|---|---|
| **D** A computer services firm. | **E** Something with more responsibility. | **F** Next year | **G** Just north of Paris. |
| **H** A manager. | **I** In Western Europe and North America. | **J** It specializes in software for banks. | **K** About 1.5 million per year. |
| **L** Customer Services. In the head office. | **M** Yes, in Accounts. | **N** At an insurance firm in Switzerland. | **O** In the head office. |
| **P** I have a big office. | **Q** A new training programme for telephone staff. | **R** My office closed. | **Congratulations** You got the job! |

Presenting your company

## 12 WORD PUZZLE

Complete the word puzzle. The first letter of each word is given.

1. We have 500 m² of office _____.
2. How many different _____ does your company make?
3. The money you receive for doing your job.
4. You manufacture things in this building.
5. Computer programs.
6. How many people does your company _____?
7. A type of power or energy.
8. We offer a full _____ of services.
9. They have production _____ all over the world.
10. These people are very important for companies.

# 3 Exchanging information

## 1 GETTING INFORMATION

A customer is calling a company for information. Put the conversation in order 1–13. See the example.

A  I see. Which part of the country do you live in? ___

B  Hello, I'd like some information about your rotary engines. ___

B  Sorry, is that Gil, G-I-L? ___

A  No, sixteen. One six. And the phone number is 942 361 854. ___

B  Well, I live in Spain and I'm trying to find a supplier who stocks your machines. ___

B  854, OK. Thanks very much for your help. ___

A  Good afternoon. GPS International Sales. How can I help you?  _1_

B  In the north, near Santander. ___

B  Sorry, did you say sixty, six oh? ___

A  Thank you for calling. Goodbye. ___

A  One moment, I'll just check. Yes, there is a supplier in Santander. The name is Hermanos Gil. ___

A  Yes, that's right. And the address is Cisneros 16. ___

A  Certainly. What would you like to know exactly? ___

## 2 CHECKING DETAILS

*Language reference 14, p56*

Complete A's sentences in this conversation. See the example.

A  QuickMail. Can ¹ _I help you?_

B  Yes, this is Pangloss Incorporated in Boston. Would it be possible to fax me a copy of your latest price list?

A  Yes, of course. Could I ² _____?

B  Yes, it's 617 731 8033.

A  Sorry, did ³ _____ double-oh three?

B  No, oh double-three

A  OK, I've got that. And could you ⁴ _____?

B  Yes, it's Peter Schuster.

A  Is ⁵ _____ S-H-U-S-T-E-R ?

B  No, it's S-**C**-H.

A  And what ⁶ _____ again?

B  Pangloss. That's P-A-N-G-L-O-S-S.

A  OK, Mr Schuster. I'll send that to you right away. Thank you ⁷ _____.

B  Goodbye.

Exchanging information

# 3 VOCABULARY

Complete the text by using the letters in brackets to make words. See the example. The first letter of each word is given.

### Westpoint Centre

The perfect venue for your conference or [1] _trade_ (drate) fair.

## Facilities
Westpoint Centre provides 2,000 m² of [2] e_____ (obixenhiti) space for your fair, a large congress hall with 1,200 [3] s_____ (atses), and six [4] m_____ (emigten) rooms for 50–120 people.

## Accommodation
Our three partner hotels are all within five minutes' walk of the Westpoint Centre. They all offer [5] d_____ (coindusts) of 10% for [6] r_____ (sarterinevos) of twenty rooms or more.

## Travel
Our partners Transworld Travel can offer special prices on [7] f_____ (sthilfg) from 30 European airports and arrange car, minibus, or helicopter [8] t_____ (lartev) to and from the Westpoint Centre. Travel [9] i_____ (sunanirec) is offered free of charge.

For further [10] i_____ (otomifranin) call 0800 564 784 and ask for a copy of our [11] b_____ (crborehu), or visit our [12] w_____ (bitewes) at www.westpointctr.net.

Exchanging information

25

## 4 JOB RESPONSIBILITIES

**Language reference 12, p55**

a   Here are some questions about your job. Complete the questions with *Do you have to* or *Can you*. See the example.

1   <u>Do you have to</u> work long hours?
2   _____ work at weekends?
3   _____ take holiday when you want?
4   _____ travel a lot in your job?
5   _____ use your work phone for personal calls?
6   _____ work late in the evening?
7   _____ go home for lunch?
8   _____ wear what you want to work?
9   _____ use English in your job?

b   Now answer the questions in **a** for your own job. See the examples.

1   <u>Yes, I do. I usually work 45–50 hours a week./No, I don't. I work part-time.</u>
2   _____
3   _____
4   _____
5   _____
6   _____
7   _____
8   _____
9   _____

**Exchanging information**

## 5 STRANGE LAWS

Match the laws below with pictures **a–h**. Then complete each law with one of these words. See the example.

can   can't   have to   has to   don't have to

# Unusual laws from around the world

1  In Ottawa, Canada, you ¹ *can't* eat ice cream in Bank Street on a Sunday.

2  In Victoria, Australia, light bulbs ² _____ be changed by qualified electricians. You can't do it yourself.

3  In Antibes, France, you ³ _____ take photos of police officers or police vehicles.

4  In Haifa, Israel, you ⁴ _____ take bears to the beach (but maybe you can if they're wearing a swimming costume!).

5  In Italy, the police ⁵ _____ arrest a man if he's wearing a skirt.

6  In Scotland, it is illegal to be drunk in possession of a cow. So if a Scotsman wants to spend an evening at the pub, he ⁶ _____ leave his cow at home!

7  In Singapore, shops ⁷ _____ sell chewing gum. If the police see you eating chewing gum on an underground train, they ⁸ _____ ask you to pay a fine.

8  In South Korea, police ⁹ _____ refuse gifts of money from car drivers, but they ¹⁰ _____ declare all money they receive.

a   b   c   d

e   f   g   h

Exchanging information

# 6 PRODUCT SPECIFICATIONS

## *HardTop mats*

**Key features**
HardTop mats offer the possibility of superb graphics. The most popular choice for promotional mats in the UK.

**Composition**
Ultra-strong 0.4 mm surface chosen for its good mouse performance and ability to provide strong, bright colours. These mats are extremely long-lasting.

**Foam base**
Black 3 mm EPDM foam is standard. The extra thickness offered by 5 mm foam is also popular.

**Standard sizes**
155 mm x 200 mm ('Mini-Mat')
200 mm x 235 mm (the most popular)
200 mm x 260 mm
Circle diameter 200 mm
Ellipse 200 mm x 235 mm
A3 desk/counter mat 297 mm x 420 mm
A2 desk/counter mat 420 mm x 595 mm

## *UltraThin HardTop mouse mats —*

*so thin, the mat is just part of your desk*

**Key features**
Around 0.5 mm thick, this exceptionally thin version of the best-selling HardTop mat is effectively part of the top of a desk.

**Sizes**
As for HardTop mats. The 'Mini-Mat' and 200 mm x 235 mm sizes are very light – only 18 g and 27 g respectively.

**See-through and Photo mats**
See-through mats are HardTop mats with a clear, liftable flap. The transparent top material is fixed to the base on one side, allowing the rest of the top to lift up. Good for customers who wish to use their own, frequently changing, inserts.
Photo Mats have a pocket in the foam into which users can put their own photographs.

*All other details as for HardTop mats.*

**Business card mats**
A HardTop mat in which you can put your business card. Ideal for sales representatives to give to their customers. The mat has a small pocket along one of the short edges. This can be made to fit the size of your business card.

*All other details as for HardTop mats.*

| | |
|---|---|
| **insert** | something, usually a document, that is placed in something else |
| **version** | a different form or type of a particular product |

Exchanging information

a   Read the product specifications opposite and say if these statements are true (T) or false (F).

1   HardTop mats are very strong. (_____)
2   The UltraThin HardTop mat is only half a millimetre thick. (_____)
3   The foam base of HardTop mats is available in three different thicknesses. (_____)
4   You can change the photo or picture in See-through mats as often as you want. (_____)
5   The pocket in Business card mats is only available in one size. (_____)
6   The most popular mat is 200 mm long. (_____)
7   It's possible to buy a round mat. (_____)
8   The Business card mat is good as a gift. (_____)

b   Find the opposites of these words in the text opposite. See the example.

1   bad            *good*
2   thick          _____
3   opaque         _____
4   weak           _____
5   dark (in colour) _____
6   bottom         _____
7   least favourite _____
8   heavy          _____

c   Complete the questions. See the example.

1   How *many* different sizes are there?
    There are seven.
2   How _____ is the UltraThin 'Mini-Mat'?
    Only 18 g.
3   How _____ is the most popular model?
    235 mm.
4   How _____ do the mouse mats cost?
    It depends how many you want to order.
5   How _____ is the A3 mat?
    297 mm.
6   How _____ is the foam base of HardTop mats?
    Either 3 mm or 5 mm.
7   _____ is the base of the mouse mat made of?
    Foam.

**Exchanging information**

## 7 COMPANY PERKS

Find two-word expressions in the list and match them with definitions **1–9**. See the example.

| annual | language | company | **hours** | ticket | health |
| salary | overtime | casual | insurance | plan | bonus |
| training | car | season | pension | monthly | clothes |

1  If you do these at work, you are usually paid more money.   _overtime_   _hours_
2  Your employer may give you this if you drive a lot for your job.   _____   _____
3  You buy this if you travel regularly on public transport.   _____   _____
4  You need this to protect you if you become ill.   _____   _____
5  This is a way of saving money for when you are older.   _____   _____
6  If you need English for your job, you ask for this.   _____   _____
7  You receive this every four weeks for the work you do.   _____   _____
8  You can wear these if your company is very relaxed.   _____   _____
9  You receive this at the end of the year if you've done well.   _____   _____

## 8 DESCRIBING PRODUCTS

Choose a title for each column **1–4** of the table from the list below, then complete the rest of the table. See the example.

| Shape | Colour | Dimension | Material |

| 1 _____ | 2 _____ | 3 _____ | 4 _____ |
|---|---|---|---|
| black | height | plastic | oval |
| white | thickness | metal | conical |
| green | depth | cardboard | triangular |
| 5 _yellow_ | 6 _wi_ | 7 _wo_ | 8 _re_ |
| 9 _pu_ | 10 _we_ | 11 _pa_ | 12 _sq_ |
| 13 _b_ | 14 _le_ | 15 _gl_ | 16 _ro_ |

**Exchanging information**

Language reference 11, p55

## 9 WORD PUZZLE

Find the opposites of these words in the word grid. The words can read across → or down ↓. See the example.

1  colder         *hotter*
2  more difficult _____
3  lighter        _____
4  older          _____
5  more expensive _____
6  better         _____
7  more unhealthy _____
8  faster         _____
9  higher         _____
10 richer         _____

| h | o | t | t | e | r | q | j | f | c |
|---|---|---|---|---|---|---|---|---|---|
| e | f | h | g | a | d | r | o | h | h |
| a | w | o | r | s | e | g | l | e | e |
| l | l | c | j | i | z | w | s | a | a |
| t | f | r | v | e | y | v | l | v | p |
| h | k | o | s | r | m | h | o | i | e |
| i | x | p | n | p | l | o | w | e | r |
| e | s | e | p | o | o | r | e | r | m |
| r | y | o | u | n | g | e | r | z | r |

Language reference 11, p55

## 10 THEN AND NOW

Compare life in your country now with twenty years ago. Choose adjectives from the list. See the example.

easy   expensive   short   low   light   good   poor   long
difficult   bad   cheap   **high**   heavy   rich

1  Office rents              *are higher*
2  The working week          _____
3  Unemployment              _____
4  Traffic in cities         _____
5  The student population    _____
6  Taxes                     _____     … than twenty years ago.
7  Petrol                    _____
8  Working abroad            _____
9  People                    _____
10 Life                      _____

Exchanging information

31

## 11 TRANSPORT STATISTICS

**Language reference 11, p55**

Complete the texts using the correct form of the adjectives from the lists. See the example. You can use the adjectives more than once.

| short | quiet | crowded | **long** |

| Road networks (km) | | Traffic density (vehicles per km) | |
|---|---|---|---|
| 1 USA | 6,307,584 | 1 Hong Kong | 276 |
| 2 India | 3,319,644 | 2 Taiwan | 245 |
| 3 Brazil | 1,980,000 | 3 Lebanon | 205 |

The USA has [1] _the longest_ road network in the world. India's road network is [2] _____ than the USA's but [3] _____ than Brazil's. In terms of traffic, it is Hong Kong which has the [4] _____ roads, with 276 vehicles per kilometre. Taiwan's roads are [5] _____ than Hong Kong's, but [6] _____ than Lebanon's.

| high | low | popular | poor |

| Car owners (cars per 1,000 people) | | | |
|---|---|---|---|
| Top 3 | | Bottom 3 | |
| 1 Lebanon | 732 | 1 Somalia/Central African Rep. | 0.1 |
| 2 Brunei | 576 | 2 Armenia/Mozambique | 0.3 |
| 3 Luxembourg | 566 | 3 Bangladesh | 0.4 |

In the Middle East the car is [7] _____ form of transport. Lebanon has [8] _____ number of car owners in the world, followed by Brunei, where the number of car owners is a little [9] _____ than in Luxembourg. Not surprisingly, it is in [10] _____ countries of the world that we find [11] _____ number of car owners. Bangladesh has only 0.4 car owners per 1,000 people, and Armenia and Mozambique are slightly [12] _____ than that, at 0.3. But it is Somalia and the Central African Republic which have [13] _____ number of car owners, with only 0.1 per 1,000 people.

Exchanging information

## 12 WORD PARTNERS

a   Match verbs **1–10** with the words in **a–j**. See the example.

1   make — **a** *a holiday/a break/English lessons*
2   ask for     **b** a trade fair/an exhibition/a party
3   pay         **c** sales/the quality/your results
4   *take*      **d** an order/the bill/the size
5   rent        **e** a birthday/a new contract/your company's 50th anniversary
6   celebrate   **f** information/a discount/more time
7   check       **g** a booking/a phone call/a comparison
8   book        **h** a stand/equipment/a car
9   organize    **i** a deposit/the balance/the bill
10  improve     **j** your flight/a hotel room/a holiday

b   Now complete these sentences with expressions from **a**. See the example. Use each verb once only.

1   I always *take a holiday* in June when the weather's good and the roads aren't too busy.
2   We want a 20% deposit, then you have to _____ the week before.
3   We're asking all our customers how we can _____ of our service.
4   We're going for a drink to _____ with IBM.
5   It costs a lot to _____ at a trade fair or exhibition.
6   If you're not happy with the price, why don't you _____?
7   I've organized your hotel: you just need to _____ to Oslo.
8   Why don't we _____ to celebrate the launch of our new product range?
9   It's difficult to _____ between the products because we don't have the prices.
10  Make sure you _____ before you pay – they made a mistake last time.

Exchanging information

33

# Getting things done

## 1 GETTING THINGS DONE

A manager is organizing an 'open evening' to launch his company's new range of products. Here is a list of things he has done or has to do.

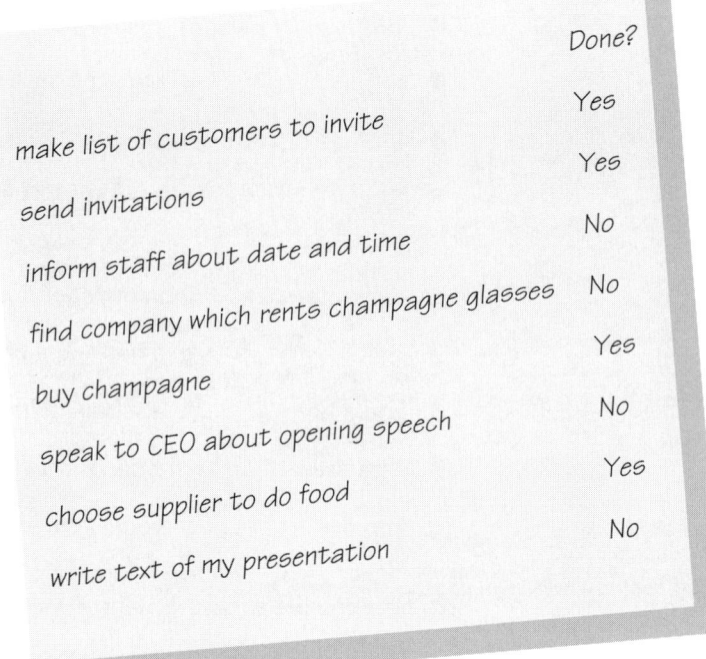

**Language reference 6 and 17, pp 53 and 57**

a   Complete the questions and answers. See the example.

1   Has he _made_ a list of customers to invite?   _Yes, he has._
2   Has he _____ the invitations?   _____
3   Has he _____ a company which rents champagne glasses?   _____
4   Has he _____ the champagne?   _____
5   Has he _____ to the CEO about the opening speech?   _____
6   Has he _____ a supplier to do the food?   _____
7   Has he _____ the text of his presentation?   _____

b   Write sentences to describe what things he has done. See the example.

1   _He's made a list of customers to invite._
2   _____
3   _____
4   _____

c   Write sentences to say what he hasn't done yet. See the example.

1   _He hasn't informed the staff about the date and time yet._
2   _____
3   _____
4   _____

Getting things done

34

## 2 A BUSY MONTH

Language reference 3, 6, and 17, pp 52–3 and 57

Renée Liebermann is a senior manager in an international retailing group. Read her report and put the verbs in brackets into the Present perfect or Simple past. See the example.

I ¹ __have had__ a very busy time this month. I ² _____ (go) on business trips to the Far East, Eastern Europe, and South America and I ³ _____ (attend) more than fifty meetings.
From the 2ⁿᵈ to the 6ᵗʰ I ⁴ _____ (be) in Japan to open a new store in Tokyo and to meet local managers there. We ⁵ _____ (open) twelve stores in the Far East this year, and we ⁶ _____ (not/finish) yet!
Two weeks ago I ⁷ _____ (fly) to Budapest, Zagreb, and Krakow to talk to potential partners there. We ⁸ _____ (not/decide) anything yet, but I think the long-term prospects for Eastern Europe are very good.
Last week I ⁹ _____ (travel) to Buenos Aires and Bogota, where we ¹⁰ _____ (launch) our sales operations three years ago. The first two years ¹¹ _____ (be) rather difficult, but last year we ¹² _____ (spend) $30 million on an advertising campaign in Latin America. I'm pleased to report that sales ¹³ _____ (rise) by more than 20% so far this year.

## 3 VOCABULARY PUZZLE

Rearrange the letters to make words which match the definitions. See the example.

1 You can employ them, pay them, or recruit them.
   F A F S T          __staff__

2 A supplier can send it, and a customer can check it or pay it.
   C I E N O V I      _____

3 Someone can make it, and you can accept it or refuse it.
   O N I T A T I N I V   _____

4 You can open it, look for addresses on it, or update it.
   A B E S T A D A    _____

5 You can ask a supplier for it, read it, and find product information in it.
   H O C U R B E R    _____

6 A caller can leave it, and you can receive it and give it to someone.
   S E G A S M E      _____

7 You write them, someone checks them, then they are read aloud at the next meeting.
   S U N I T E M      _____

Getting things done

## 4 APOLOGIES, EXCUSES, AND OFFERS

**Language reference 13, pp 55–6**

a   Find four apologies (A), four excuses (E), and four offers (O). See the examples.

1   I'm afraid our usual warehouse manager is away this week.   ( E )
2   Would you like to make an official complaint to the rail company?   ( O )
3   Yes, it's out of order. I'm sorry about that.   ( A )
4   Shall I send someone to have a look at it?   (___)
5   I called the telecom engineer but he hasn't come yet .   (___)
6   I'm sorry to hear that. Production speed isn't normally a problem.   (___)
7   I'm really sorry. We don't usually make mistakes like that.   (___)
8   It's because there are engineering works on the line.   (___)
9   It's probably because the machine's still new.   (___)
10  I'm very sorry about the delay.   (___)
11  You can use my personal phone if it's urgent.   (___)
12  I'll dispatch the rest of them today.   (___)

b   Now use phrases from **a 1–12** to complete B's sentences in the conversations below. In each dialogue B makes an apology, an excuse, and an offer. See the example.

**1**

A   I can't use your pay phone.

B   _Yes, it's out of order. I'm sorry about that._ (Apology) _I called the telecom engineer but he hasn't come yet._ (Excuse) _You can use my personal phone if it's urgent._ (Offer)

A   No, that's OK, thanks. It can wait until I get home.

**2**

A   We ordered two hundred, but you only sent us one hundred.

B   _____

A   OK, thanks. I look forward to receiving them tomorrow.

**3**

A   You told me it produced up to 3,000 units per minute.

B   _____

A   Yes, please , if you could.

**4**

A   It's the third time this week this train has been late.

B   _____

A   Yes, I think I will. How do I do it?

Getting things done

36

## 5 MUZAK!

a  Read the article below quickly. What is 'muzak'?

# How to complain about muzak

Ordinary daily life has never been noisier. It has now become acceptable to play muzak in a reception room, a bus or a taxi. Muzak is also now often found in doctor's waiting areas and in hospitals.

In recent years, the quality of muzak has changed from a quiet background sound to loud, aggressive noise. We have to listen to muzak in restaurants, supermarkets and public places. We have no choice in this: it is a commercial strategy to make us spend more money.

In a recent poll, 17% of people chose muzak as 'the thing they hate most about modern life' (34% of people hated it, only 30% liked it, and 36% were indifferent). A survey by Gatwick Airport in 1994 showed that 43% of its respondents disliked its muzak.

There is now a website that will help you to protest about the increasing use of muzak by national and international companies in Britain. It will provide addresses, telephone numbers, e-mail addresses and website addresses so that you can quickly and easily make a complaint.

## Radio presenter opposes muzak

A BBC Radio presenter recently took direct action in a Sheffield hotel, asking for the muzak to be turned off. When he was told by the management that the customers liked it, he went round and asked them and found that they all agreed with him. The manager finally agreed to turn it off when the radio presenter said he wanted to leave.

| | |
|---|---|
| **aggressive** | violent |
| **background** | (of music, noise, etc.) something you can hear but is not too loud |
| **indifferent** | don't feel strongly about something |

b  Now read the article again and say if these sentences are true (T) or false (F).

1  The writer wants to encourage people to complain about muzak.  (___)
2  Surveys and polls have indicated that most people hate muzak.  (___)
3  Muzak is noisier than before.  (___)
4  About one in six people dislike muzak more than anything else in modern life.  (___)
5  Muzak stops people from spending money.  (___)
6  The radio presenter wanted the hotel manager to reduce the volume of the music.  (___)
7  The radio presenter left the hotel.  (___)

Getting things done

## 6 RECRUITING A NEW MANAGER

**Language reference 15, p56**

a  What things do you have to do to recruit a new manager? Match verbs **1–9** with expressions **a–i**. (The steps are not in the normal order.) See the example.

| 1 | invite | a | the best four candidates |
| 2 | inform | b | a job description |
| 3 | write | c | the best candidate the post |
| 4 | advertise | d | *15–20 candidates for a first interview* |
| 5 | ask | e | salary and other conditions |
| 6 | choose | f | the other three candidates that they don't have the job |
| 7 | decide on | g | the post in the newspaper |
| 8 | arrange | h | the candidates' employers for a reference |
| 9 | offer | i | a second interview |

b  You are responsible for recruiting a new manager. Put the steps in **a** in order and write a description using *we should …* and *we need to …* . See the example.

1  First, *we need to write a job description.*
2  Then, _____
3  After that, _____
4  Next, _____
5  Then, _____
6  Following this, _____
7  Next, _____
8  After that, _____
9  Finally, _____

## 7 THERE'S WORK TO BE DONE

What do you need to do in your department in the next three to six months? Write sentences using *We need to …* or *We should …* . See the examples.

1  *We need to update our customer database.*
2  *We should start preparing the new brochure.*
3  _____
4  _____
5  _____
6  _____

Getting things done

38

## 8 WHO'S DOING WHAT?

**Language reference 15, p56**

Complete the conversations using an expression from **A** with an expression from **B**. See the example.

| A | B |
|---|---|
| Could you … <br> Shall I … | call you back a little later? <br> prepare some figures? <br> phone the restaurant? <br> **phone them for you?** <br> ask them to wait? <br> check them for me? <br> contact some other suppliers? <br> offer them some coffee? |

1. A  We need to contact the printers about the new brochure.
   B  *Shall I phone them for you?*
   A  Yes, please. That would be helpful.

2. A  The IT department needs to know which computers aren't working.
   B  I must finish this report. _____
   A  Yes, OK. I'll do that.

3. A  I can hear you're very busy. _____
   B  Yes, please, if you don't mind. In about ten minutes?

4. A  They make good-quality products, but their prices are high.
   B  _____
   A  No, thanks, that's not necessary. I'll ask my secretary to do it.

5. A  We should inform the directors about the latest sales results.
      _____
   B  Yes, of course. Do you want them just for April, or for March too?

6. A  They want to have lunch outside. _____
   B  Yes, sure. Where do you want to take them?

7. A  Hello, Mrs Gardener. Your visitors are waiting in reception.
   B  I'll be there in five minutes, Sophie. _____
   A  Yes, of course, Mrs Gardener. _____
   B  No, that's not necessary. I have some here for them.

Getting things done

39

## 9 TIME EXPRESSIONS

*Language reference 9, p54*

a  Complete this description of a new product launch by choosing the correct prepositions in *italics*.

8th May

### Progress report on launch of RX23

We are now confident that everything will be ready [1] *at/by* the middle of June for the official product launch. We tested the prototype successfully [2] *in/from* the beginning of March [3] *to/at* the end of April. We also installed the production machinery [4] *at/in* April, and production will start [5] *in/on* 15th May. The marketing department started work on the advertising material [6] *in/at* the beginning of this month, and they're having a final meeting about this [7] *in/on* Monday [8] *to/at* 2 p.m. They have confirmed that the final copy will be finished [9] *at/by* 24th May, a full week before the start of the sales campaign.

b  Now use the information above to decide what each letter in this chart refers to. See the example.

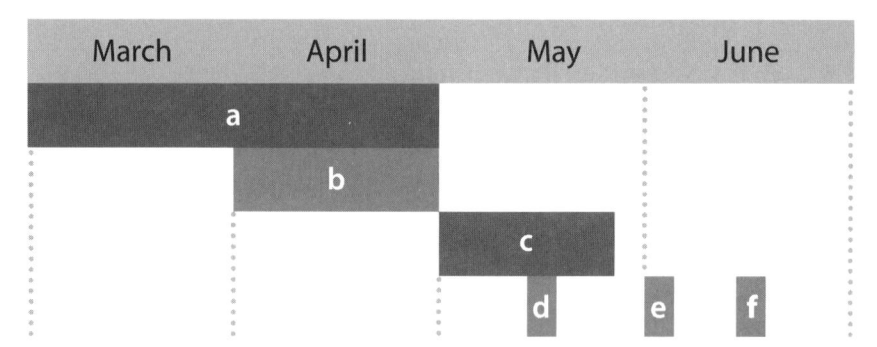

| March | April | May | June |
|---|---|---|---|
| a | | | |
| | b | | |
| | | c | |
| | | d | e | f |

__f__  official product launch
____  preparation of advertising
____  start of production
____  testing of prototype
____  start of sales campaign
____  installation of production machinery

Getting things done

40

## 10 CROSSWORD

Complete the crossword.

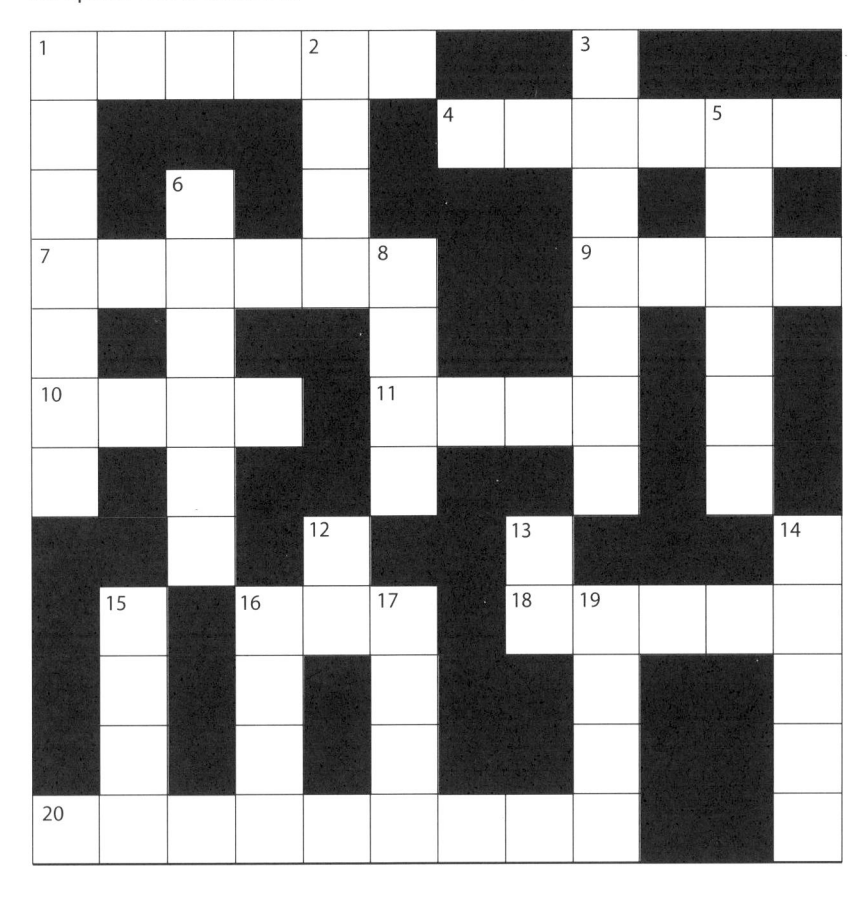

**Across**
1. We need to u_____ our database by adding this year's new clients.
4. Not very difficult, not easy, but f_____ difficult.
7. If you're not happy with the goods, you can ask the shop for a r_____.
9. Would you like a t_____ of the company before our meeting?
10. We can offer you a special d_____ on group orders.
11. A piece of work to be done.
16. The opposite of *high*.
18. If someone complains to you, you o_____ to do something to make them happy.
20. They a_____ their services in the newspaper every week.

**Down**
1. A new improved version of the same product.
2. Can I just check that you said eighty and not eigh_____?
3. An error.
5. To introduce a product on the market for the first time.
6. I'm a_____ we don't have that product in stock.
8. When can you confirm the delivery d_____?
12. The opposite of *come*.
13. Good morning, sir. What can I _____ for you?
14. Could I have a copy of your brochure and p_____ list, please?
15. Can you s_____ us another copy of your invoice?
16. The opposite of *early*.
17. Could you w_____ just one moment, please – I'll check on my computer.
19. When you don't have to pay for something, it's f_____.

**Getting things done**

41

## 11 CHECKING INFORMATION

Language reference 14, p56

A purchasing manager is calling a potential supplier. Complete his questions with words from the list below. Then match questions **1–8** with answers **a–h**.

> that   suppose   check   tell   says   there   right   confirm

1 Your brochure _____ that you have sales offices all over Europe.
2 Is _____ an office in Italy?
3 So I _____ you can send us a sales rep fairly quickly?
4 Could you _____ that the prices in your brochure include delivery?
5 And you can always deliver within 48 hours. Is that _____ ?
6 I couldn't access your website. Can I just _____ the address?
7 Is _____ all in small letters?
8 Could you _____ me who you work with in Italy?

a It's www.digipress.com.
b Yes, in fact we have two.
c That's right. But for orders of €500 or more.
d Yes, we can, but only if we have the items in stock.
e Yes, it is.
f I'm afraid I can't give you the names of our customers.
g Yes, if you give me your details, someone will call you by the end of the day.
h That's right. We now have a network of seventeen branches.

## 12 CORRECTING INFORMATION

You are responsible for selling the 'Revo Plus' mobile Internet organizer. Answer the customer's questions in **1–8** opposite by beginning with one of these expressions. See the example.

> Yes, that's right. It ...   No, in fact it ...

Getting things done

1  A  I suppose it's not very heavy.
   B  <u>Yes, that's right. It only weighs 200 g.</u>

2  A  And it's very small and compact?
   B  _____

3  A  Is it true that it has a colour screen?
   B  _____

4  A  I imagine you have to change the batteries quite often?
   B  _____

5  A  Can you confirm that it has a loudspeaker?
   B  _____

6  A  And somebody told me it has a small keyboard – only 81 keys?
   B  _____

7  A  You can write on the screen with a special pen. Is that right?
   B  _____

8  A  And do you have to pay extra for an external power supply?
   B  _____

## 13 CONFIRMING PROGRESS

Complete this extract from a meeting. The first letter of each word is given. See the example.

A  I've asked you here because we ¹ <u>need</u> to review the work done on the new warehouse. We ² s_____ also decide today on a final completion date. Tom, can you just ³ c_____ that all the external work has been completed.

T  Yes, we've finished the walls and the roof, but we haven't started the inside ⁴ y_____ .

A  Serena, ⁵ h_____ you ordered the new lifting equipment?

S  No, I wanted to talk to you about the pricing. ⁶ S_____ I show you the quotation I've received?

A  Well, maybe not now. ⁷ C_____ you come to my office after the meeting and I'll ⁸ c_____ the figures with you?

S  Sure.

A  Dillon, what about the floor of the warehouse? ⁹ H_____ the builder contacted you?

D  Yes, he called me last week, but I wasn't here. I'm ¹⁰ a_____ I haven't had time to call him back. I'm ¹¹ s_____ about that.

A  Well, could you call him after this meeting?

D  Yes, ¹² I_____ do that.

Getting things done

# 5 Planning ahead

## 1 OFFICIAL APPOINTMENTS

A government minister (A) is talking to his Private Secretary (B) about his appointments for tomorrow. Complete the conversation with the correct form of the verbs from the list. Use the information in the appointments schedule to help you. See the example.

| see | come | visit | make | talk | **meet** | introduce |
| interview | not/come | not/send | speak | go | do |

### Appointments schedule

8.30 a.m.      meeting with Private Secretary
10.00 a.m.     radio interview with Hugh Wimple on 'Business World'
12.30 p.m.     lunch at Chamber of Commerce
               make speech on government industry statistics
3.00 p.m.      official opening of high tech business centre
               (40 TV/radio/press reporters invited)
               talk to architects
               visit centre with Managing Director
               introduction to young managers

**Language reference 2 and 5, pp 52 and 53**

A   What time ¹ _am_ I _meeting_ you tomorrow morning?
B   At 8.30. Then Hugh Wimple ² _____ you on 'Business World' at 10.
A   And when ³ _____ we _____ to the Chamber of Commerce?
B   At 12.30. You ⁴ _____ a speech after lunch.
A   Yes, I ⁵ _____ my speech writer this evening.
B   Very good.
A   What ⁶ _____ I _____ for the official opening of the business park?
B   You ⁷ _____ to the architects. Then the Managing Director ⁸ _____ the centre with you, and he ⁹ _____ you to some young managers who work there.
A   That's good. ¹⁰ _____ the big TV companies _____ for the opening?
B   Most of them, but Channel TV ¹¹ _____ a reporter.
A   It doesn't matter. It's only a small local company. ¹² _____ I _____ to any women managers in the centre? I have to think of my image with women voters.
B   Well, we invited two female directors, but they ¹³ _____ . They're away on business.
A   That's a pity.

Planning ahead

## 2 PERSONAL SCHEDULES

**Language reference 2 and 5, pp 52 and 53**

a  Match verbs **1–6** with nouns **a–f**.

1 attend          a  a holiday
2 give            b  a report
3 write           c  a visitor
4 visit           d  a conference
5 receive         e  a presentation
6 take            f  a customer

b  What are you doing in the next two weeks? Write sentences about yourself using the verbs and nouns in **a**. See the examples.

1 *I'm receiving two visitors from our biggest supplier.*
2 *I'm not writing any reports.*
3 _____
4 _____
5 _____
6 _____
7 _____
8 _____

## 3 MAKING APPOINTMENTS

**Language reference 14, p56**

Tony Harvey (A) calls Monica Di Stefano (B) to arrange a meeting for next week. Put the conversation in the correct order. See the example.

A  Yes, why not? So that's eleven on Friday, then. ___
A  Hello. Is that Monica?  _1_
B  Yes, Friday's OK. But not in the afternoon, because I'm leaving the office early. I'm going to Paris with the family for the weekend. ___
B  Yes, I think so, if we can find a time. I'm very busy next week. ___
A  That's nice. Well, is eleven o' clock OK for you? Or is that too late? ___
A  Yes, me too. What day are you free? ___
B  Great. See you next week. ___
B  How about Wednesday? ___
A  I'm sorry, Monica, but I've got meetings all day Wednesday. What about Monday afternoon? ___
B  Well, I'd prefer later in the week if possible, Tony. ___
A  I'd like to see you next week about the new production schedule. Is that possible? ___
A  Are you free on Friday? ___
B  Yes, it is.  Hello, Tony. What can I do for you? ___
B  No, that's fine. Why don't we go for a quick lunch after our meeting? ___

Planning ahead

## 4 A NEW PRODUCT

**Language reference 4 and 5, p53**

Two managers are discussing the launch of a new product. Complete the conversation with the Present continuous (e.g. *we're doing*) or the *will* form (e.g. *we'll do*) of the verbs in brackets. See the example.

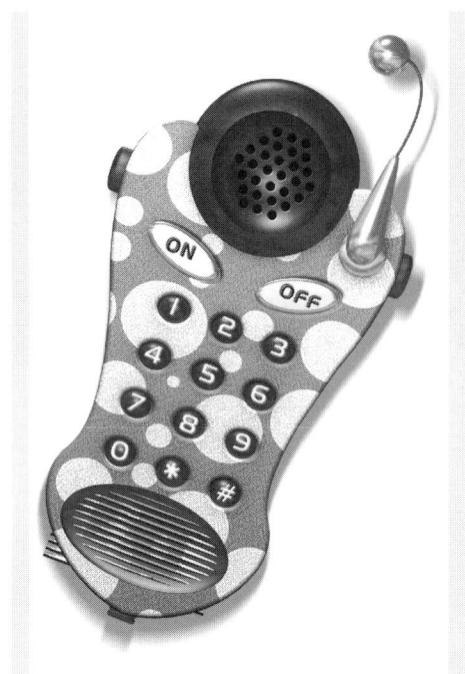

**Product: The 'FunFone'**

Marketing plan
*Launch date*: October
*Advertising*: from mid-October (TV and posters)
*Distributors*: toy shops, phone shops

Market predictions
*Customers*: parents of young children
(for their children and for themselves)
*Sales*: 30,000 before end of year

A  So when ¹ *are you launching* (you/launch) the new product?
B  In October. We think ² _____ (it/be) very popular as a Christmas present.
A  And when ³ _____ (you/begin) the advertising campaign?
B  ⁴ _____ (We/advertise) on TV from mid-October and ⁵ _____ (we/spend) €0.5 million on a poster campaign.
A  Who ⁶ _____ (your customers/be)?
B  We believe that ⁷ _____ (parents/buy) it as a toy for their children.
A  And I suppose ⁸ _____ (they/use) it to stay in contact with their children when they play outside in the street.
B  Yes, exactly.
A  How many ⁹ _____ (you/sell), do you think?
B  Well, our target is 30,000 units before the end of the year. Personally, I don't think ¹⁰ _____ (we/reach) that target. 25,000 is more realistic.
A  And where ¹¹ _____ (you/distribute) it?
B  Mainly toy shops. But also shops which sell phones and mobile phones.

Planning ahead

## 5 READING

**a** Complete the text with the phrases below.

> ... people will have to learn to live with new office technologies
> ... people will need to separate 'personal' and 'work' space
> ... more and more people will work from home
> ... home-workers will need to develop new social relationships
> ... people working at home will have to find new technical support systems

## The future of work

In the future, ¹_____, or part-time in the company and the rest of the time at home. This change in working practices will create new technological and social problems in the years to come.

First, ²_____. For the moment, many people are afraid of them. It will be important to make computers more user-friendly and to develop training to help workers respond positively to the idea of technological change.

Secondly, ³_____. As we all know, computer systems often break down, and they are often a great source of stress. It won't always be possible for companies to send a technician to people's homes. For this reason it will be important for home-workers to develop a relationship with a local computer resource centre.

Thirdly, ⁴_____ because they will have less contact with co-workers. They will have to go out and find other people living in the neighbourhood who also work from home, and establish new social contacts with them.

Finally, ⁵_____. This means that the home-worker will have to decide with his or her family which part of the house is for professional life and which part for home life. It is also important to make the distinction between 'work time' and 'personal time'. If these rules are not established, it will create a very stressful home life for all members of the family.

**b** Match words or phrases in the text with **1–8**.

1 ways of working _____
2 easy to use _____
3 courses/lessons _____
4 stop working/crash _____
5 cause of anxiety/worry _____
6 create _____
7 near your house _____
8 difference/division _____

**c** Five people are giving their opinion about different points in the text in **a**. Decide which point they are talking about and then choose the correct expression *in italics*. See the example.

1 *I think/**I don't think** it'll* be necessary because they're already very easy to use.
   <u>make computers more user-friendly</u>

2 It's a good idea, but I'm sure *it'll/it won't* work where I live. Nobody's interested in meeting new people. _____

3 I think he's right. If you don't have that rule, in a few weeks *there'll be/there won't* be papers all over the house. _____

4 I think *it'll/it won't* be really useful. People complain about new IT systems, because they're worried about their future. _____

5 I agree that *it'll/it won't* be important because it can be two or three days before someone comes and looks at it. _____

Planning ahead

47

## 6 MAKING PREDICTIONS

**Language reference 4, p53**

Make predictions using *will* or *won't*. See the example.

1 shopping on the Internet
   *Internet shopping will/won't be more popular than normal shopping.*

2 jobs in the IT industry
   _____

3 electric cars
   _____

4 air travel
   _____

5 the number of unemployed people
   _____

## 7 GIVING ADVICE

**Language reference 15, p56**

Some of your colleagues have problems. Give them advice, using the expressions given. Use the ideas in the list to help you, and add extra information. See the example.

| advertise the post | leave a message | ask the IT department |
| ask your secretary | explain more clearly | **take a break** |
| leave work | see your doctor | |

1 My eyes get very tired looking at the computer all day.
   Why don't you *take a break every 45 minutes* ?

2 I can't finish this report because the phone's always ringing.
   How about _____ ?

3 My computer has crashed three times this morning.
   Why don't you _____ ?

4 His phone's still engaged and his cell phone's switched off.
   You could _____

5 The traffic's always terrible when I drive home in the evening.
   How about _____ ?

6 Nobody in the company is interested in the new job.
   You could _____

7 I have difficulty sleeping at night.
   How about _____ ?

8 My secretary doesn't understand me.
   Why don't you _____ ?

Planning ahead

## 8 PLANS AND INTENTIONS

*Language reference 5, p53*

A CEO is giving a presentation about his company's new strategy. Complete his presentation with the correct form of the verb pairs from this list. Use the CEO's notes to help you. See the example.

plan/launch    hope/increase    plan/double    go/join    plan/recruit
**go/do**    hope/have    plan/maintain    go/reduce

PLANS
- prices on existing products: 10%
- new product engineer (from AKM)
- R & D spending x 2

OBJECTIVES
- 1 new product before end of year
- 2nd product ready next year
- 22% market share this year (same as last year)
- 30% market share within five years

As you know, our competitors AKM have launched three new products this year. These products are technically better than ours and, on average, 5% cheaper. So what ¹ _are_ we _going to do_ about this situation?

First of all, to stay cheaper than our competitors, we ² _____ the prices of our present products by 10%. Secondly, we ³ _____ a new product engineer. He is currently working with AKM, but he ⁴ _____ our team at the end of this month. Finally, we ⁵ _____ the R & D budget from €2.5 m to €5 m.

So what exactly are our objectives? First of all, the company ⁶ _____ one new product before the end of this year, and the R & D department ⁷ _____ a second one ready for the beginning of next year. In terms of results, we ⁸ _____ our present market share of 22% this year, and we ⁹ _____ our share of the market to 30% within 5 years.

Planning ahead

## 9 WORD-BUILDING

a  Complete the table. See the example.

| Verb | Noun |
|------|------|
| build | building |
|  | recruitment |
|  | production/product |
|  | installation |
|  | improvement |
|  | complaint |
|  | target |

b  Now use words from **a** to complete these sentences.

1  We plan to _____ a new factory in Philadelphia.
2  The Customer Service Department has received a lot of _____ about the new model.
3  How many units do you _____ every year?
4  We hope to see a big _____ in quality soon.
5  What kind of customers are you going to _____?
6  The _____ of the new system will probably take about two days.
7  The Personnel Manager is reponsible for _____.

## 10 SAYING GOODBYE

**Language reference 13, p55–6**

A manager (A) is saying goodbye to a visitor (B). Complete the conversation with appropriate phrases. See the example.

A  Thank ¹ *you for coming* to see us.
B  Thank you ² _____ me.
A  It was a pleasure. And I thought your talk was most interesting.
B  I'm glad ³ _____ it.
A  So when are you going back?
B  My plane's at four this afternoon. I'm seeing an old friend for lunch before I go.
A  That's nice. Well, have ⁴ _____.
B  Thanks very much.
A  And have ⁵ _____ back to London.
B  Thanks. And see you in March when you come to us.
A  Yes. I look ⁶ _____. I'll call you in a couple of weeks to confirm the details.
B  Great. Speak ⁷ _____ then. Goodbye.

Planning ahead

50

## 11 WORD CHAIN

Complete the puzzle. The last letter of each word is the first letter of the next. All the words appear in the Student's Book.

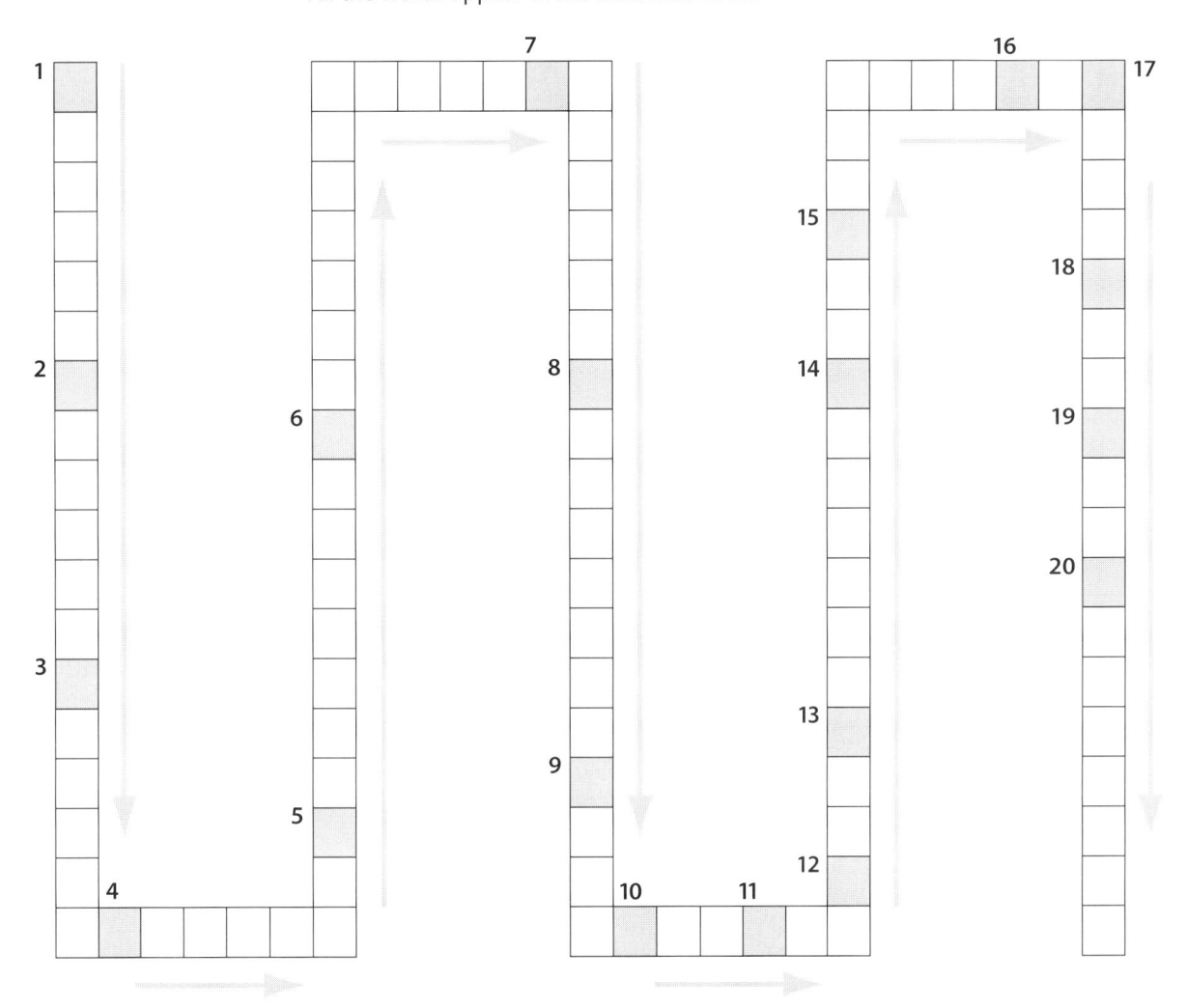

1 When can you _____ the goods to our factory?
2 To take on new employees.
3 Financial or sales objectives.
4 Computer programs.
5 The opposite of *cheap*.
6 Theatre, cinema, concerts, etc.
7 Volume of sales in £, $, €, etc.
8 A decrease.
9 To give customers what they want, you have to know their _____.
10 Opposite of *buy*.
11 You use this to go up and down in a building.
12 A guided visit of a company, town, etc.
13 One half of R & D.
14 Where is the _____ office of your company?
15 If you sell only in your country, you're in the _____ market.
16 Chief Executive Officer.
17 I'm calling about your _____ reference PW 247.
18 How much does it cost to _____ a car for the day?
19 Hello, Juan. How was your _____ to Rome?
20 The building where your company is located.

Planning ahead

51

# Language reference

## 1 PRESENT SIMPLE

### Form

The Present simple is formed from the infinitive. The third person (he/she/it) form ends in -s or -es. Negatives and questions are formed using *do* or *does*.

| AFFIRMATIVE | |
|---|---|
| I/You/We/They | work. |
| He/She/It | work**s**. |

| NEGATIVE | |
|---|---|
| I/You/We/They | don't work. |
| He/She/It | do**es**n't work. |

| QUESTIONS | | |
|---|---|---|
| Do | I/you/we/they | work? |
| Do**es** | he/she/it | work? |

### Use

The Present simple is used:

a  to talk about actions and activities that don't change.
   *Motorola **produces** electronic components.*
   *I always **go** to work by car.*
   *Who do you **work** for?*

b  to talk about travel timetables.
   *My train **leaves** at 14.32.*
   *What time **does** the next plane **arrive**?*

## 2 PRESENT CONTINUOUS

### Form

The Present continuous is formed by using the verb *to be* and the *-ing* form of the main verb.

| AFFIRMATIVE | | |
|---|---|---|
| I | am ('m) | working. |
| You / We / They | are ('re) | working. |
| He / She / It | is ('s) | working. |

| NEGATIVE | | |
|---|---|---|
| I | am not ('m not) | working. |
| He/She/It | is not (isn't) | working. |
| You/We/They | are not (aren't) | working. |

| QUESTIONS | | |
|---|---|---|
| Am | I | working? |
| Is | he/she/it | working? |
| Are | you/we/they | working? |

### Use

The Present continuous is used:

a  to talk about something that is happening at the moment of speaking.
   *Don't go into his office – **he's talking** on the phone.*

b  to talk about present activities that are only temporary.
   *I work for a computer services firm. This week **I'm working** in the IT department of a large bank.*

c  to talk about a situation that is changing.
   *Companies **are becoming** more interested in profit than people.*

d  to talk about personal arrangements for the future.
   ***I'm preparing** my presentation this evening. What **are you doing**?*

## 3 SIMPLE PAST

### Form

The Simple past of regular verbs is formed by adding *-ed* to the infinitive. Negatives and questions are formed using *did* and the infinitive.

| AFFIRMATIVE | |
|---|---|
| I/You/He/She/It/We/They | work**ed**. |

| NEGATIVE | |
|---|---|
| I/You/He/She/It/We/They | **didn't** work. |

| QUESTIONS | | |
|---|---|---|
| **Did** | I/you/he/she/it/we/they | work? |

**Note:** Many common verbs have irregular forms in the Simple past. See the list on page 57.

## Use

The Simple past is used to talk about completed actions or events in the past.
He **created** the company in 1952.
When I was a student, I **worked** in bars to earn extra money.
Where did you go last week?

## 4 FUTURE WITH *WILL*

### Form

*Will* is followed by the infinitive of the verb (without *to*).

**AFFIRMATIVE**

I/You/He/She/It/We/They     will work.

**NEGATIVE**

I/You/He/She/It/We/They     will not (won't) work.

**QUESTIONS**

Will     I/you/he/she/it/we/they     work?

### Use

*Will* is used:

a   to make predictions about the future.
I think **we'll have** better results next year.
I heard that the weather **won't be** very good tomorrow.

b   to express decisions you make at the time of speaking.
A: *Can I take a message?*
B: *No thanks.* **I'll** *call back later.*

## 5 OTHER WAYS OF TALKING ABOUT THE FUTURE

a   If we are talking about personal arrangements, we use the Present continuous.
**I'm leaving** for New York tomorrow, but Pat **is staying** in the office.

b   To talk about a personal or company project, we use *going to*.
**I'm going to start** looking for a new job.
When **are they going to do** a new market study?

c   *Plan to* is more often used to talk about company projects or objectives.
**They plan to open** the new office in June.
Where **do they plan to sell** the new product?

d   We use *hope to* to describe projects where the result is less sure.
We **hope to double** our turnover in the next three years.
**I hope to come** and see you next week, but it depends on my work.

## 6 PRESENT PERFECT

### Form

The Present perfect is formed with the verb to *have* and the past participle form of the main verb. There is a list of irregular past participles on page 57.

**AFFIRMATIVE**

| I/You/We/They | have ('ve) | worked. |
| He/she/it | has ('s) | worked. |

**NEGATIVE**

| I/You/We/They | have not (haven't) | worked. |
| He/She/It | has not (hasn't) | worked. |

**QUESTIONS**

| Have | I/you/we/they | worked? |
| Has | he/she/it | worked? |

### Use

The Present perfect is used to talk about past actions that have a relation with the present. For example, we use it:

a   to talk about progress.
**We've sent** the new brochure to all our customers.
**He hasn't finished** the report yet, but he's going to do it today.

b   to talk about periods of time that are not finished. It is often used with *today, this week, this year*, etc.
**I've called** them three times today, but they are never there.
How many weeks holiday **have you taken** this year?

Language reference

## 7 THE VERB *TO BE*

### Form

In the Present simple and Simple past, the verb *to be* doesn't take *do*, *does*, or *did* in questions and negative sentences.

#### AFFIRMATIVE

*Present simple*

| | | |
|---|---|---|
| I | am ('m) | here. |
| You/We/They | are ('re) | here. |
| He/She/It | is ('s) | here. |

*Simple past*

| | | |
|---|---|---|
| I/He/She/It | was | here. |
| You/We/They | were | here. |

#### NEGATIVE

*Present simple*

| | | |
|---|---|---|
| I | am not ('m not) | here. |
| You/We/They | are not ('re not/aren't) | here. |
| He/She/It | is not ('s not/isn't) | here. |

*Simple past*

| | | |
|---|---|---|
| I/He/She/It | was not (wasn't) | here. |
| You/We/They | were not (weren't) | here. |

#### QUESTIONS

*Present simple*

| | | |
|---|---|---|
| Am | I | here? |
| Are | you/we/they | here? |
| Is | he/she/it | here? |

*Simple past*

| | | |
|---|---|---|
| Was | I/he/she/it | here? |
| Were | we/you/they | here? |

## 8 PRESENT SIMPLE PASSIVE

### Form

The Present simple passive is formed with the present of the verb *to be* and the past participle.

#### AFFIRMATIVE

| | | |
|---|---|---|
| I | am ('m) | employed. |
| You/We/They | are ('re) | employed. |
| He/She/It | is ('s) | employed. |

#### NEGATIVE

| | | |
|---|---|---|
| I | am not ('m not) | employed. |
| You/We/They | are not ('re not/aren't) | employed. |
| He/She/It | is not ('s not/isn't) | employed. |

#### QUESTIONS

| | | |
|---|---|---|
| Am | I | employed? |
| Are | you/we/they | employed? |
| Is | he/she/it | employed? |

### Use

The passive is used:

a to focus on the action and not the person doing the action.
   Active: **We sell** these products in Europe.
   Passive: These products **are sold** in Europe.
b to talk about processes.
   The parts **are made** in the Far East, then they **are transported** to Germany.

## 9 TIME EXPRESSIONS

Note the use of the prepositions below:

| | |
|---|---|
| **in** | (months/years/seasons) *in July, in 2001, in summer* |
| **on** | (dates/days) *on September 15th, on Friday* |
| **at** | (times) *at 5.30 p.m., at midday* |
| **from … to** | (times/days/dates/months/years) *from 1950 to 1985, from 2.00 to 4.30* |
| **by** | (times/days/dates/months/years) *by August, by the end of the week* |

## 10 COUNTABLE AND UNCOUNTABLE NOUNS

a Countable nouns have a plural form, usually with *-s* or *-es*. They are things that we can count.
   *six computers, four companies, two different solutions*
b Note these irregular countable nouns:
   *one person/man/woman*
   *two people/men/women*
c Uncountable nouns have no plural form. They are things that we can't count. For example, we can't say ~~two moneys~~. Common uncountable nouns include:
   *money, information, equipment, experience, time, food*

Language reference

**d** We use *How many …?* to ask questions with countable nouns and *How much …?* for uncountable nouns.
How **many** companies are there in the group?
How **much** experience does he have?

## 11 COMPARISONS

### Form

All adjectives have a comparative and a superlative form for making comparisons.

**a** Adjectives of one syllable:
long     long**er**     the long**est**
old     old**er**     the old**est**

**b** Adjectives ending in *–y*:
easy     eas**ier**     the easi**est**
healthy     health**ier**     the healthi**est**

**c** Adjectives of two or more syllables:
expensive    **more** expensive    the **most** expensive
crowded    **more** crowded    the **most** crowded

**d** Irregular forms:
good     better     the best
bad     worse     the worst
far     further     the furthest

### Use

**a** To compare two things, we use the comparative form of the adjective followed by the word **than**.
He's young**er than** me.
It's **more** expensive **than** last year.

**b** To compare three things or more, we use the superlative form of the adjective.
He's the young**est** person in the company.
It's the **most** expensive hotel in town.

## 12 MODAL VERBS

Modal verbs have different meanings in different situations.

**a** *Can* and *can't* are used to say what is permitted (in your company, job, etc.).
I **can** take my holidays when I want.
You **can't** come in if you don't have a security pass.

**b** *Can* and *could* are used to make requests.
**Can/Could** you spell your name, please?
**Can/Could** I call you back later?

**c** *Could* is also used to suggest ideas or give advice.
We **could** go and eat now.
You **could** try to call him at home.

**d** *Shall* is used to offer help or suggest action.
That bag's very heavy. **Shall** I take it for you?
It's 12.30. **Shall** we stop for lunch now?

**e** *Have to* and *not have to* are used to say what is necessary and not necessary.
They can describe general situations (e.g. job responsibilities) or specific situations (e.g. work to be done now).
I **have to** work 39 hours a week, but I **don't have to** work at weekends.
He **has to** write the report before the end of this week, but he **doesn't have to** send it.

**f** *Need to* and *should* are used to say what is necessary in a specific situation. *Need to* is a little stronger than *should*.
We **need to** send the quotation today, or we'll lose the order.
I think we **should** launch the product this month, if possible.

## 13 SOCIAL EXPRESSIONS

Here are some common social expressions, with appropriate responses.

**a** Introducing yourself:
A: *Hello. (Can I introduce myself.) My name's …*
B: *How do you do?/Pleased to meet you.*

**b** Saying hello:
A: *Hello, Juan. How are you?*
B: *Fine, thanks, and you?/Very well, and you?*

**c** Asking someone to do something:
A: *Can/Could you … (help me?)*
B: *Yes, of course./Yes, certainly./I'm afraid I can't, because …*

**d** Asking to do something:
A: *Can/Could I … (ask you a question?)*
B: *Yes, of course./Yes, go ahead./I'm afraid not, because …*

**e** Inviting:
A: *Can I offer you …/Would you like … (a coffee)?/Would you like to (visit the factory)?*
B: *Yes, please./That would be nice./No, thanks.*

**f** Offering help:

Language reference

A: Shall I (do it for you)?/I'll … (do it for you).
B: Thanks very much./That's kind of you./No, that's OK, thanks.

**g** Saying sorry:
A: I'm sorry (I'm late)./I'm sorry about that.
B: It's no problem./It doesn't matter.

**h** Giving bad news
A: I'm sorry, but … /I'm afraid … (I can't come).
B: I'm sorry to hear that./That's a pity.

**i** Thanking:
A: Thank you very much./Thanks for … (your help).
B: You're welcome./It's a pleasure.

**j** Saying goodbye:
A: Have a good … (holiday/weekend/trip back).
B: Thanks. (You too.)
A: See you … (tomorrow/next week/soon).
B: Yes, (I look forward to it./I hope so.).

## 14 TELEPHONE EXPRESSIONS

**a** Introducing yourself:
This is (Cristina).
(Robert Crupp) speaking.

**b** Asking for someone:
Can/Could I speak to (Antonia), please?
I'd like to talk to (Ben Ali), please.

**c** Taking /leaving a message:
(caller)
Can/Could I leave a message?
Can/Could you ask him/her to call me back?
Can/Could you tell him/her I called?
(person called)
Can/Could I take a message?
I'll give him/her the message.

**d** Asking for more details:
Can/Could I have your (name)?
Can/Could you give me your (phone number)?

**e** Checking and correcting information:
Can/Could I just check your (personal details)?
Your name is Keller. Is that right?
Could you confirm that (it's £45 a night)?
Could you say that again?
Sorry. Did you say (thirty or thirteen)?
Sorry. Was that (A or E)?

**f** Making appointments:
When are you free?
Are you free on (Thursday)?

I'm sorry, but/I'm afraid (that's not possible).
How about (Friday)?
Is (2.15 p.m.) OK?
So that's (Friday) at (2.15), then.

**g** Finishing the call:
(It was) nice talking to you.
Thank you for calling.
Thanks for your help.

## 15 MEETING EXPRESSIONS

**a** Giving opinions:
I think (it's a good idea).
I don't think (it's a good idea).
I agree (with you).
I disagree/I don't agree.

**b** Making suggestions:
Why don't we (open a new office)?
We could (find a new supplier).
How about (launching a new product)?

**c** Deciding on priorities:
First we need to/should (research the market).
Then/Next/Finally we need to/should …

**d** Deciding on responsibilities:
A: Shall I (prepare a report)?
B: Yes, please. And could you (send it to the CEO)?

## 16 NUMBERS

| Cardinal numbers | | Ordinal numbers* | |
|---|---|---|---|
| 1 | one | 1st | first |
| 2 | two | 2nd | second |
| 3 | three | 3rd | third |
| 4 | four | 4th | fourth |
| 5 | five | 5th | fifth |
| 6 | six | 6th | sixth |
| 7 | seven | 7th | seventh |
| 8 | eight | 8th | eighth |
| 9 | nine | 9th | ninth |
| 10 | ten | 10th | tenth |
| 11 | eleven | 11th | eleventh |
| 12 | twelve | 12th | twelfth |
| 13 | thirteen | 13th | thirteenth |
| 14 | fourteen | 14th | fourteenth |
| 15 | fifteen | 15th | fifteenth |
| 16 | sixteen | 16th | sixteenth |
| 17 | seventeen | 17th | seventeenth |
| 18 | eighteen | 18th | eighteenth |

Language reference

| 19 | nineteen | 19th | nineteenth |
| 20 | twenty | 20th | twentieth |
| 21 | twenty-one | 21st | twenty-first |
| 30 | thirty | 30th | thirtieth |
| 31 | thirty-one | 31st | thirty-first |
| 40 | forty | | |
| 50 | fifty | | |
| 60 | sixty | | |
| 70 | seventy | | |
| 80 | eighty | | |
| 90 | ninety | | |
| 100 | a hundred | | |
| 1,000 | a thousand | | |
| 1,000,000 | a million | | |

\* Ordinal numbers are used for dates, e.g. *June 5 = the fifth of June* or *June the fifth*

**More complex numbers**

| 1.67 | one point six seven |
| 79% | seventy-nine per cent |
| 4.5 bn | four point five (four and a half) billion |
| $164 | a hundred and sixty-four dollars |
| 5,241 | five thousand two hundred and forty-one |

## 17 COMMON IRREGULAR VERBS

| Infinitive | Simple past | Past participle |
|---|---|---|
| be | was/were | been |
| become | became | become |
| begin | began | begun |
| break | broke | broken |
| bring | brought | brought |
| build | built | built |
| buy | bought | bought |
| catch | caught | caught |
| choose | chose | chosen |
| come | came | come |
| cost | cost | cost |
| cut | cut | cut |
| deal | dealt | dealt |
| do | did | done |
| draw | drew | drawn |
| drink | drank | drunk |
| drive | drove | driven |
| eat | ate | eaten |
| fall | fell | fallen |
| feel | felt | felt |
| find | found | found |
| fly | flew | flown |
| forget | forgot | forgotten |
| freeze | froze | frozen |
| get | got | got |
| give | gave | given |
| go | went | gone |
| grow | grew | grown |
| have | had | had |
| hear | heard | heard |
| hide | hid | hidden |
| hit | hit | hit |
| hold | held | held |
| keep | kept | kept |
| know | knew | known |
| lead | led | led |
| leave | left | left |
| lend | lent | lent |
| let | let | let |
| lose | lost | lost |
| make | made | made |
| mean | meant | meant |
| meet | met | met |
| pay | paid | paid |
| put | put | put |
| read | read | read |
| ride | rode | ridden |
| ring | rang | rung |
| rise | rose | risen |
| say | said | said |
| see | saw | seen |
| sell | sold | sold |
| show | showed | shown |
| shut | shut | shut |
| sit | sat | sat |
| sleep | slept | slept |
| speak | spoke | spoken |
| spend | spent | spent |
| stand | stood | stood |
| steal | stole | stolen |
| swim | swam | swum |
| take | took | taken |
| teach | taught | taught |
| tell | told | told |
| think | thought | thought |
| throw | threw | thrown |
| understand | understood | understood |
| wake | woke | woken |
| wear | wore | worn |
| win | won | won |
| write | wrote | written |

Language reference

# Answer key

## 1 OUT AND ABOUT

**1 Getting to know you**
2 e What do you do?
3 a Where is your company based?
4 g What does your company do?
5 b What nationality are you?
6 f Where do you work?
7 c What languages do you speak?

**2 Answering questions**
2 I'm a/an (your job title).
3 It's based in (name of town and/or country).
4 It produces/We produce (type of products).
   or It sells/We sell (type of products or services).
5 I'm (nationality).
6 I work in (name of town).
7 I speak (languages).

**3 Countries and nationalities**
2 Switzerland/Swiss
3 Germany/German
4 Holland/Dutch
5 Spain/Spanish
6 Japan/Japanese
7 Korea/Korean
8 USA/American

**4 Questions of nationality**
2 do/Portuguese
3 does/Swedish
4 is/Canadian
5 does/Polish
6 do/Spanish

**5 Airport services**
a
2g 3f 4e 5a 6b 7c 8d
b
1 gift shop
2 first aid
3 left luggage
4 men's toilets
5 information desk
6 check-in area
7 car hire
8 departure lounge

**6 Describing a factory**
a
1 preparation area
2 equipment store
3 main production area
4 cutting machines
5 testing area
6 packing room
b
2 next to/behind
3 next to
4 right
5 between
6 opposite
7 over

**7 Conference details**
2 Is
  Yes, there is.
3 Are
  No, there aren't.
4 do
  They leave at half past ten/ten-thirty.
5 do
  They leave from the front of the hotel.
6 does
  It closes at half past two/two-thirty.
7 is
  It's next to the hotel.
8 does
  It arrives at five to three/two fifty-five.

**8 Alphabet soup**
Like *play*: H, A, J
Like *be*: G, V
Like *bed*: X
Like *fly*: Y I
Like *no*: O
Like *you*: U, W
Like *star*: R

**9 Telephone requests**
2 Can I have the name of
3 Could you spell that
4 Can I speak to
5 Can I take
6 Could you give me
7 could you repeat

**10 Invitations**
3 to read/to look at or to see
4 to use/to borrow
5 to come/to call
6 a coffee/a tea
7 to come/to go
8 a copy

**11 Social responses**
1c 2e 3f 4g 5a 6b 7h 8d

### 12 Job responsibilities
1 reports to
2 responsible for
3 manages
4 in charge of
5 manages
6 reports to

### 13 You and your job
*Suggested answers*
1 I'm the Product Manager/I'm an engineer/I'm the Marketing Director, etc.
2 I'm in charge of training/finding new customers/a team of ten people, etc.
3 I'm also responsible for improving quality/welcoming visitors/sales, etc.
4 I report to the CEO/the Sales Director/the Production Manager, etc.

### 14 Management culture
Answers for column A (Sweden)
1T 2T 3F 4T 5T 6F 7T

### 15 Crossword
| Across | Down |
|---|---|
| 1 seat | 1 Sales |
| 2 for | 3 opens |
| 5 engineer | 4 produces |
| 7 based | 6 go |
| 11 see | 8 an |
| 13 arrive | 9 Is |
| 14 and | 10 head |
|  | 12 six |

## 2 PRESENTING YOUR COMPANY

### 1 Trading areas
1 Portugal
2 Poland/Hungary
3 Saudi Arabia/Egypt
4 Thailand/Vietnam
5 USA/Canada
6 Argentina/Brazil

### 2 Company activities
a
1e 2f 3h 4a 5g 6b 7c 8d
b
2 produces
3 publishes
4 has
5 provides or produces
6 develops/designs
7 sells
8 constructs
9 operates

### 3 Saying numbers
a
2 22,000
3 800,000
4 6.61 bn or 6,610,000,000
5 22.5 or 22½
b
2 two hundred and twenty thousand
3 eight point seven nine billion
4 eight thousand three hundred
5 twenty-six point five one billion

### 4 Asking about quantity
a
1 d
2 g many
3 a much
4 b many
5 h much
6 f much
7 c many
8 e much
b
Students' own answers.

### 5 Company departments
a
1 Marketing
2 Production
3 Advertising
4 Packaging
5 Customer Service
b
1 Purchasing
2 Dispatch
3 Marketing
4 Sales
5 Advertising
6 Customer Accounts

### 6 Present activities
a
3 starts
4 shows
5 provide
6 pass
7 are
8 have
9 are selling
10 are opening
11 is becoming
12 is talking
13 has

Answer key

**b**
3 What do petrol stations always provide?
4 What are more and more petrol stations selling?
5 What are big supermarket groups doing?
6 Who is FTV talking to?
7 What other plans does the company have?

**7 Active or passive?**
2 give
3 pack
4 is confirmed
5 sold
6 buys
7 is
8 Do
9 don't/isn't

**8 Shopping online**
2 are checked
3 are sent to the warehouse
4 are found (by the picker)
5 are packed (by the packer)
6 is put in the box
7 is created
8 an e-mail is sent (or you are sent an e-mail) to confirm the delivery time (and the package is put in the post)

**9 To be or not to be**
1 Is
2 is
3 are
4 am/'m
5 were
6 was
7 was
8 Were
9 weren't
10 wasn't
11 was/is
12 Are
13 aren't
14 isn't
15 are/'re

**10 Personal history**
**a**
accepted /ɪd/
worked /t/
returned /d/
joined /d/
negotiated /ɪd/
published /t/
studied /d/ or /ɪd/
started /ɪd/

**b**
go – went
be – was/were
write – wrote
teach – taught
have – had
begin – began
leave – left

**c**
1 studied
2 worked
3 returned
4 taught
5 began
6 joined
7 was
8 left
9 wrote
10 thought
11 had
12 published
13 started
14 accepted
15 went
16 negotiated

**11 A job interview**
**a**
2 What sort of job are you looking for?
3 When did you join your present company?
4 Where is your company based?
5 What does your company do?
6 Where are its products sold?
7 Which department do you work in?
8 What are you working on at the moment?
9 Where did you work before?
10 Why did you leave your last job?
**b**
1D 2E 3B 4G 5J 6I 7L 8Q 9N 10R

**12 Word puzzle**
1 space
2 products
3 salary
4 factory
5 software
6 employ
7 nuclear
8 range
9 sites
10 customers

# 3 EXCHANGING INFORMATION

**1 Getting information**
Order of sentences (from top to bottom):
5, 2, 8, 11, 4, 12, 1, 6, 10, 13, 7, 9, 3

**2 Checking details**
2 take/have your fax number
3 you say
4 tell/give me your name
5 that
6 was (the name of) your company
7 (very much) for calling

**3 Vocabulary**
2 exhibition
3 seats
4 meeting
5 discounts
6 reservations
7 flights
8 travel
9 insurance
10 information
11 brochure
12 website

**4 Job responsibilities**
**a**
2 Do you have to
3 Can you
4 Do you have to
5 Can you
6 Do you have to
7 Can you
8 Can you
9 Do you have to/Can you

Answer key

**b**

*Suggested answers*
2 Yes, I do, but not every weekend.
 / No, I don't.
3 Yes, I can.
 /No, I can't. I have to take at least three weeks in the summer.
4 Yes, I do. I have to drive about 500 km a week.
 /No, I don't. I always work in my office.
5 Yes, I can, but I can't make too many calls.
 /No, I can't.
6 Yes, I do. I often have to work until 7 or 8 p.m.
 /No, I don't. I usually finish at 5.30 p.m.
7 Yes, I can. I live very near the office.
 /No, I can't. I don't have time.
8 Yes, I can.
 /No, I can't. I have to wear a shirt and tie/a business suit.
9 Yes, I do (Yes, I can). I receive visitors from time to time.
 /No, I don't (No, I can't).

## 5 Strange laws
a Haifa, Israel
b Italy
c South Korea
d Scotland
e Singapore
f Australia
g Antibes
h Ottawa, Canada

2 have to
3 can't
4 can't
5 can/have to
6 has to
7 can't
8 can/have to
9 don't have to
10 have to

## 6 Product specifications
**a**
1 T
2 T
3 F (there are two sizes – 3 mm and 5 mm)
4 T
5 F (it can be made in special sizes for your business card)
6 F (it's 200 mm wide, but 235 mm long)
7 T
8 T

**b**
2 thin
3 transparent/see-through
4 strong
5 bright
6 top
7 most popular
8 light

**c**
2 heavy
3 long
4 much
5 wide
6 thick
7 What

## 7 Company perks
2 company car
3 season ticket
4 health insurance
5 pension plan
6 language training
7 monthly salary
8 casual clothes
9 annual bonus

## 8 Describing products
1 colour
2 dimension
3 material
4 shape
6 width
7 wood
8 rectangular
9 purple
10 weight
11 paper
12 square
13 brown/blue
14 length
15 glass
16 round

## 9 Word puzzle
2 easier
3 heavier
4 younger
5 cheaper
6 worse
7 healthier
8 slower
9 lower
10 poorer

## 10 Then and now
*Suggested answers*
2 is shorter or longer
3 is higher or lower/better or worse
4 is heavier or lighter/better or worse
5 is higher or lower
6 are higher or lower
7 is more expensive or cheaper
8 is easier or more difficult
9 are richer or poorer
10 is easier or more difficult/better or worse

## 11 Transport statistics
2 shorter
3 longer
4 most crowded
5 quieter or less crowded
6 more crowded
7 the most popular
8 the highest
9 higher
10 the poorest
11 the lowest
12 lower
13 the lowest

## 12 Word partners
**a**
1g 2f 3i 5h 6e 7d 8j 9b 10c
**b**
2 pay the balance
3 improve the quality
4 celebrate the new contract
5 rent a stand
6 ask for a discount
7 book your flight
8 organize a party
9 make a comparison
10 check the bill

Answer key

# 4 GETTING THINGS DONE

## 1 Getting things done
**a**
2 sent/Yes, he has.
3 found/No, he hasn't.
4 bought/Yes, he has.
5 spoken/No, he hasn't.
6 chosen/Yes, he has.
7 written/No, he hasn't.

**b**
2 He's sent the invitations.
3 He's bought the champagne.
4 He's chosen a supplier to do the food.

**c**
2 He hasn't found a company which rents champagne glasses yet.
3 He hasn't spoken to the CEO about the opening speech yet.
4 He hasn't written the text of his presentation yet.

## 2 A busy month
2 have been/'ve been
3 have attended/'ve attended
4 was
5 have opened/'ve opened
6 haven't finished
7 flew
8 haven't decided
9 travelled
10 launched
11 were
12 spent
13 have risen

## 3 Vocabulary puzzle
2 invoice
3 invitation
4 database
5 brochure
6 message
7 minutes

## 4 Apologies, excuses, and offers
**a**
Apologies (A): 6, 7 and 10
Excuses (E): 5, 8 and 9
Offers (O): 4, 11 and 12

**b**
2 Apology: 7
　Excuse: 1
　Offer: 12
3 Apology: 6
　Excuse: 9
　Offer: 4
4 Apology: 10
　Excuse: 8
　Offer: 2

## 5 Muzak!
**a**
Muzak is recorded music that is played in restaurants, supermarkets and other public places.

**b**
1T 2F 3T 4T 5F 6F 7F

## 6 Recruiting a new manager
**a**
2f 3b 4g 5h 6a 7e 8i 9c

**b**
*Suggested answers (different orders are possible*
*We need to/should ...*
2 decide on salary and other conditions
3 advertise the post in the newspaper
4 invite 15–20 candidates for an interview
5 choose the best four candidates
6 arrange a second interview
7 ask the candidates' employers for a reference
8 offer the best candidate the post
9 inform the other three candidates that they don't have the job

## 7 There's work to be done.
Students' own answers.

## 8 Who's doing what?
2 Could you check them for me?
3 Shall I call you back a little later?
4 Shall I contact some other suppliers?
5 Could you prepare some figures?
6 Could you phone the restaurant?
7 Could you ask them to wait?/
　Shall I offer them some coffee?

## 9 Time expressions
**a**
1 by　　　6 at
2 from　　7 on
3 to　　　8 at
4 in　　　9 by
5 on

**b**
a testing of prototype
b installation of production machinery
c preparation of advertising
d start of production
e start of sales campaign

## 10 Crossword
**Across**
1 update　　11 task
4 fairly　　　16 low
7 refund　　18 offer
9 tour　　　20 advertise
10 deal

Answer key

**Down**

| | | | |
|---|---|---|---|
| 1 | upgrade | 13 | do |
| 2 | teen | 14 | price |
| 3 | mistake | 15 | send |
| 5 | launch | 16 | late |
| 6 | afraid | 17 | wait |
| 8 | date | 19 | free |
| 12 | go | | |

## 11 Checking information

| | | | | |
|---|---|---|---|---|
| 1 h | says | 5 d | right |
| 2 b | there | 6 a | check |
| 3 g | suppose | 7 e | that |
| 4 c | confirm | 8 f | tell |

## 12 Correcting information

*Suggested answers*

2 Yes, that's right. It's only 157 mm (in length) by 79 mm (in width) by 18 mm (in thickness).
3 No, in fact it has a black and white (monochrome) screen.
4 No, in fact it has built-in rechargeable batteries.
5 Yes, that's right. It has a 23 mm loudspeaker.
6 No, in fact it has a keyboard with only 53 keys.
7 Yes, that's right. It has a special pen called the 'Revo Plus'.
8 No, in fact it includes a 6.0 V external power supply.

## 13 Confirming progress

| | | | | |
|---|---|---|---|---|
| 2 | should | 8 | check |
| 3 | confirm | 9 | Has |
| 4 | yet | 10 | afraid |
| 5 | have | 11 | sorry |
| 6 | shall | 12 | I'll |
| 7 | could | | |

# 5 PLANNING AHEAD

## 1 Official appointments

2 is interviewing
3 are, going
4 are making
5 am seeing/'m seeing
6 am/doing
7 are talking/'re talking
8 is visiting
9 is introducing/'s introducing
10 Are, coming
11 isn't sending
12 Am, speaking
13 aren't coming

## 2 Personal schedules

**a**
1d 2e 3b 4f 5c 6a
**b**
Students' own answers.

## 3 Making appointments

Order of sentences (from top to bottom):
13, 1, 10, 4, 11, 5, 14, 6, 7, 8, 3, 9, 2, 12

## 4 A new product

2 it'll be/it will be
3 are you beginning
4 We are advertising/We're advertising
5 We are spending/We're spending
6 will your customers be
7 parents will buy
8 they will use/they'll use
9 will you sell
10 we'll reach/we will reach
11 are you distributing

## 5 Reading

**a**
1 more and more people will work from home
2 people will have to learn to live with new office technologies
3 people working at home will have to find new technical support systems
4 home-workers will need to develop new social relationships
5 people will need to separate 'personal' and 'work' space

**b**
1 working practices
2 user-friendly
3 training
4 break down
5 source of stress
6 establish or develop
7 in the neighbourhood/local
8 distinction

**c**
2 it won't/establish new social contacts with people working from home.
3 there'll be/decide which parts of the house are for professional and home life.
4 it'll/develop training to help workers respond positively to technological change.
5 it'll/develop a relationship with a local customer resource centre.

Answer key

## 6 Making predictions
*Suggested answers*
2 The number of jobs in the IT industry will increase.
3 Electric cars won't replace petrol cars.
4 Air travel won't become much cheaper.
5 The number of unemployed people will stay the same or rise.

## 7 Giving advice
*Suggested answers*
2 asking your secretary to take your calls
3 ask the IT department to look at it
4 leave a message on his cell phone
5 leaving work a little earlier
6 advertise the post in the newspaper
7 seeing your doctor and asking for some pills
8 explain things to her more clearly

## 8 Plans and intentions
2 're going/are going to reduce
3 plan to recruit
4 's going/is going to join
5 plan to double
6 plans to launch
7 hopes to have
8 plan to maintain
9 hope to increase

## 9 Word building
**a**
The verbs are: recruit, produce, install, improve, complain, target
**b**
1 build
2 complaints
3 produce
4 improvement
5 target
6 installation
7 recruitment

## 10 Saying goodbye
2 for having/for inviting
3 you liked/you enjoyed
4 a nice/a pleasant lunch
5 a good/safe journey/trip
6 forward to it/that
7 to you soon/in a couple of weeks

## 11 Word chain
1 deliver
2 recruit
3 targets
4 software
5 expensive
6 entertainment
7 turnover
8 reduction
9 needs
10 sell
11 lift
12 tour
13 research
14 head
15 domestic
16 CEO
17 order
18 rent
19 trip
20 premises

**Answer key**